PROGRESSIVE
STRATEGY FOR THE
TOEIC® L&R TEST

600点を目指すTOEIC® L&R TESTへのストラテジー

Emiko MATSUMOTO

Kentaro NISHII

Sam LITTLE

JN062929

 SEIBIDO

photographs by　写真提供
Emiko Matsumoto　松本恵美子
©iStockphoto.com

音声ファイルのダウンロード／ストリーミング

CD マーク表示がある箇所は、音声を弊社 HP より無料でダウンロード／ストリーミングすることができます。下記 URL の書籍詳細ページに音声ダウンロードアイコンがございますのでそちらから自習用音声としてご活用ください。

http://seibido.co.jp/ad606

PROGRESSIVE STRATEGY FOR THE TOEIC® L&R TEST

Copyright © 2021 by Emiko MATSUMOTO, Kentaro NISHII, Sam LITTLE

All rights reserved for Japan.
No part of this book may be reproduced in any form
without permission from Seibido Co., Ltd.

はじめに

　あなたが今までにたくさんの時間を英語学習に費やしてきたとします。文法の知識もある程度ついてきましたし、リスニングの練習もしてきました。動画でネイティブが話す英語を含んだトークや映画、洋楽を動画で視聴することもできますし、英語を楽しむ方法も知っています。そろそろ実際に日常会話もビジネスでも英語が使えるだろうと思った頃、駅で外国人に英語で話しかけられます。せっかく英語を話すチャンスなのに、つい焦って、相手が何を言っているのかわからず、頭が真っ白になってしまった。などといった経験はありませんか。

　言葉を使ってコミュニケーションをとることは時として難しいものです。「これを言おう」と準備して身構えていても相手が予想外の発言をしてきたから、会話が思わぬ方向に進んでしまった。というのはよくあることです。特に相手が仕事上の付き合いであったり、あまり話したことがなかったりする人なら、会話の方向性が予測できないことも多いでしょう。適切なコミュニケーションをとるには、相手の言っていることの意味を考え、その上で、どのように応答するのがベストなのかを臨機応変に選んでいかなければなりません。反対に、毎日話をする仲の良い相手なら、お互いに築き上げた信頼関係を踏まえて、相手の思考パターンがわかるので、朝の挨拶代わりに、短いフレーズ、例えば "Did you see it?"「見た！？」と言ったとしても、相手に言いたいことが伝わることがあります。

　TOEIC で求められているのは、まさにこのような、会話の流れをとらえたコミュニケーション能力です。主にビジネスでのコミュニケーションを想定して問題作成されていますが、基本的には、相手との会話の流れ、ビジネスの展開や、メールやその応答の流れを理解することが不可欠な能力です。

皆さんがこれから受験するTOEICは現在世界160ヶ国で実施されている、グローバルな英語能力試験です。14,000の企業・教育機関で利用されており、職場で必要とされる英語力の判定基準として確立されてから、すでに30年以上が経過しています。リスニングセクション100問（45分間）、リーディングセクション100問（75分間）、約2時間の試験によってビジネスコミュニケーション能力を客観的に測定することができます。

　そのTOEICの対策用教科書である本書では文法知識だけではなく、英文を瞬時に把握し、応答のパターンを理解して、コミュニケーション能力を養いつつ、得点力をアップしてゆきます。英語の一語一語を訳すのではなく、英文の意味や流れをとらえて解答する能力を身につけることを願って執筆しています。

　本書は全15章から成っており、第1章から第14章の各章に総合テーマを設け、第15章は小テストとなっています。全ての章でPart 1からPart 7までの練習をすることができます。Part 3やPart 4では図表を含む問題を含み、第5、6、12章ではPart 7でダブルパッセージ、第7、13、14章ではPart 7でトリプルパッセージを扱っています。

　作成にあたり、1章〜15章のPart 1、Part 2、Part 3、Part 5、トピック別単語、表現集と全体の監修を松本が、Part 4、Part 6、Part 7を西井が、全文の英文校閲をLittleが担当しました。

　本書を効果的に活用され、TOEICスコアアップのための総合的な英語力を身につけられることを心より祈っております。

著者代表　松本恵美子

Contents

本 書 の 特 徴

　本書はTOEICテストを攻略する基礎力と応用力を身につけることを目的に作成しました。授業時間で問題に慣れ、解答のコツを身につけながら実践問題に親しむことができます。2016年から変更になった新形式にも対応しています。特徴は以下のようになります。

各章の最初【Key Vocabulary】にその章で出てくる単語を16個学び、最後の【ボキャブラリーアルファ】ではその章のトピックでよく使用される単語と表現が30個リストアップされています。ボキャブラリーの力を伸ばすことでTOEICでの得点アップの効果を狙っています。

Part 1、2、3、4、5にそれぞれついている、各パートのウォーミングアップ問題で書き込み式の演習ができます。

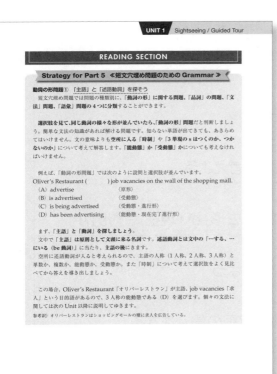

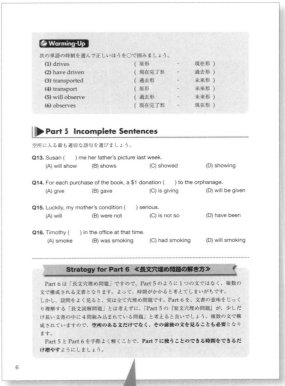

各パートが始まる前の【Strategy】では出題傾向に沿った解答のためのコツを簡単に確認することができます。特にPart 5短文穴埋め問題の前では基本的な文法事項の復習をまとめています。

全15章。1回の授業でPart 1 〜 Part 7までの実践問題を学習できます。
各章の問題数は以下のようになります。

● 第1章〜第14章

LISTENING SECTION

Part 1【2問】　Part 2【4問】　Part 3【3問】　Part 4【3問】

READING SECTION

Part 5【4問】　Part 6【4問】　Part 7【5問】

● 第15章 Mini Test

LISTENING SECTION

Part 1【4問】　Part 2【10問】　Part 3【3問】　Part 4【3問】

READING SECTION

Part 5【8問】　Part 6【4問】　Part 7【5問】

Strategy for Part 5【文法事項】

Sightseeing / Guided Tour

▶ Key Vocabulary

 1-02

この章に出てくる下の英単語の中から日本語訳に当てはまる記号を（　）に記入しましょう。
答え合わせをしたら音声を聞いて英単語を声に出して読み、つづりを書き込み覚えましょう。

●観光 / ガイドのトピックに出てくる単語

1.	称賛する	(　　)	9.	旅行日程	(　　)
2.	はしご	(　　)	10.	パンフレット	(　　)
3.	確認する	(　　)	11.	寄付	(　　)
4.	空き	(　　)	12.	孤児院	(　　)
5.	無料の	(　　)	13.	同様に	(　　)
6.	尋ねる	(　　)	14.	こうむる	(　　)
7.	案内人	(　　)	15.	周遊旅行	(　　)
8.	配る	(　　)	16.	手頃な	(　　)

a. itinerary   **b.** admire   **c.** hand out   **d.** donation

e. conductor   **f.** excursion   **g.** affordable   **h.** complimentary

i. confirm   **j.** vacancy   **k.** orphanage   **l.** likewise

m. incur   **n.** brochure   **o.** ladder   **p.** inquire

LISTENING SECTION

Strategy for Part 1 ≪写真描写問題の解き方≫

人物の写真 ①　正しい主語を予測しよう

下の Warming-Up の写真を見ながら**日本語で描写してみましょう**。

●写真には**人物１人**が写っている。　●主語は**人の可能性が高い**が、他の物かもしれない。

●一番目立つ人物は〜**している**。

● Warming-Up   1-03

音声を聞いて（　　　）内の語を穴埋めし、
正しい答えはどれか選びましょう。

(A) A (　　　　　) is running near a car.

(B) (　　) is standing with his arms folded.

(C) A (　　　　) is packing his souvenir.

(D) (　　　　　) are waving their hands.

正しい答え　(A) (B) (C) (D)

▶ Part 1　Photographs

1-04,05

英文を聞き、4つの中から最も適切な描写を選びましょう。

Q1.

Ⓐ Ⓑ Ⓒ Ⓓ

Q2.

Ⓐ Ⓑ Ⓒ Ⓓ

Strategy for Part 2　≪応答問題の解き方≫

疑問詞を聞き取ろう①

　Part 2 の設問の半分以上は 5W1H の疑問詞で始まる疑問文です。

　まず、文頭の What/When/Where/Who/Why/How を聞き取り、それを忘れないように記憶しておくことが、Part 2 を攻略するための最初の手順となります。

● Warming-Up 1-06

音声を聞いて、それぞれの疑問文の最初の一語を記入しましょう。

① (　　　　　) is going to give me the ticket?
② (　　　　　) is a good place to meet you?
③ (　　　　　) did you get that map?

▶ Part 2　Question-Response

1-07,08,09,10

設問に対する応答として、最も適切なものを選びましょう。

Q3. Mark your answer on your answer sheet.　　Ⓐ Ⓑ Ⓒ

Q4. Mark your answer on your answer sheet.　　Ⓐ Ⓑ Ⓒ

Q5. Mark your answer on your answer sheet.　　Ⓐ Ⓑ Ⓒ

Q6. Mark your answer on your answer sheet.　　Ⓐ Ⓑ Ⓒ

Strategy for Part 3 ≪会話問題の解き方≫

2人の会話問題①　設問先読みのメリット

Part 3 ではリスニングの音声が流れる前に**設問を先に読んでおく**ことが得点アップの手助けになります。設問先読みには2つのメリットがあります。

1. 正解の手掛かりとなる箇所にポイントを絞って聞くことができる。
   例）**Where is the conference taking place?** から、会議が行われている「**場所**」を聞き取ればいいことがわかる。
2. 会話文を聞く前に内容を知ることができる。
   例）**What is the man concerned about?** から「**男性が何か心配事**を抱えている」とわかる。

○ Warming-Up

次の設問を読んで、会話の内容を予測し、（　　）内に日本語を記入しましょう。

What is the woman asking about?
→女性が何かについて（　　　　　　　　　）いるとわかる。

 ## Part 3 Short Conversation 1-11,12

会話文を聞いて、各設問に対する最も適切な答えを4つの選択肢から選びましょう。

Q7. Why is the man calling?
　　(A) To borrow a book　　　　　(B) To inquire about an artist
　　(C) To reserve tickets　　　　 (D) To ask about the menu

Q8. What time will the man have dinner on March 2nd?
　　(A) 6 o'clock　　　　　　　　　(B) 7 o'clock
　　(C) 8 o'clock　　　　　　　　　(D) 9 o'clock

Q9. What is included in the tour?
　　(A) A souvenir　　　　　　　　(B) A musical
　　(C) A ceremony　　　　　　　 (D) A light meal

Strategy for Part 4 ≪説明文問題の解き方≫

トークの「種類」は冒頭でわかる！

　Part 4 はリスニングセクションの最後にあり、また 1 人の話し手が一方的に話すため、漠然と難しく感じている人が多いようです。しかし、実際はどうでしょう。例えば、2 ～ 3 名の話し手が登場し、会話がどう進んでいくかわからない Part 3 に比べ、Part 4 では**最初にトークの種類を知った上で聞く**事ができます。さらに、その**トークの種類はかなり限られている**のです。トークの前に流れる下記のようなナレーションを聞きのがさないようにしましょう。

🌀 Warming-Up 🎵 1-13

次の、説明文（トーク）に入る前に流れる音声を、スクリプトを見ながら聞きましょう。トークの種類は何でしょうか。正しいものを 1 つ選び、○で囲みましょう。

「音声スクリプト」"Questions 10 through 12 refer to the following telephone message."
（答え：会議の一部・留守電メッセージ・広告・人物紹介・公共放送・アナウンス）

▶ Part 4 Short Talk 1-14,15

説明文を聞いて、各設問に対する最も適切な答えを 4 つの選択肢から選びましょう。

Q10. Where is the talk taking place?
　　(A) In a parking lot
　　(B) In a castle
　　(C) At a bus stop
　　(D) At a station

Q11. What was handed out to the listeners?
　　(A) A train ticket
　　(B) A guide book
　　(C) A map
　　(D) An itinerary

Q12. What are the listeners advised to do?
　　(A) Return to the station
　　(B) Buy a ticket
　　(C) Take a brochure
　　(D) Pass through the gate

READING SECTION

Strategy for Part 5　≪短文穴埋め問題のための Grammar ≫

動詞の形問題①　「主語」と「述語動詞」を探そう

　短文穴埋め問題では問題の種類別に、「**動詞の形**」**に関する問題**、「**品詞**」の問題、「**文法**」問題、「**語彙**」問題の**4つに分類**することができます。

　選択肢を見て、同じ動詞の様々な形が並んでいたら、「動詞の形」問題だと判断しましょう。簡単な文法の知識があれば解ける問題です。知らない単語が出てきても、あきらめてはいけません。文の意味よりも空所に入る「**時制**」や「**3 単現の s はつくのか、つかないのか**」について考えて解答します。「**能動態**」か「**受動態**」かについても考えなければいけません。

　例えば、「動詞の形問題」では次のように設問と選択肢が並んでいます。

Oliver's Restaurant (　　　　　　) job vacancies on the wall of the shopping mall.

　(A) advertise　　　　　　　　　　〈原形〉
　(B) is advertised　　　　　　　　　〈受動態〉
　(C) is being advertised　　　　　　〈受動態・進行形〉
　(D) has been advertising　　　　　〈能動態・現在完了進行形〉

　まず、「**主語**」と「**動詞**」を探しましょう。

　文中で「主語」は原則として文頭に来る名詞です。**述語動詞とは文中の**「…**する、…にいる（be 動詞）**」**に当たり、主語の後**にきます。

　空所に述語動詞が入ると考えられるので、主語の人称（1 人称、2 人称、3 人称）と単数か、複数か、能動態か、受動態か。また「時制」について考えて選択肢をよく見比べてから答えを導き出しましょう。

　この場合、Oliver's Restaurant「オリバーレストラン」が主語、job vacancies「求人」という目的語があるので、3 人称の能動態である（D）を選びます。個々の文法に関しては次の Unit 以降に説明してゆきます。

参考訳）オリバーレストランはショッピングモールの壁に求人を広告している。

🔵 Warming-Up

次の単語の時制を選んで正しい方を〇で囲みましょう。

(1) drives	(	原形	・	現在形)
(2) have driven	(	現在完了形	・	過去形)
(3) transported	(	過去形	・	未来形)
(4) transport	(	原形	・	未来形)
(5) will observe	(	過去形	・	未来形)
(6) observes	(	現在完了形	・	現在形)

▶ Part 5 Incomplete Sentences

空所に入る最も適切な語句を選びましょう。

Q13. Susan (   ) me her father's picture last week.

    (A) will show   (B) shows   (C) showed   (D) showing

Q14. For each purchase of the book, a \$1 donation (   ) to the orphanage.

    (A) give   (B) gave   (C) is giving   (D) will be given

Q15. Luckily, my mother's condition (   ) serious.

    (A) will   (B) were not   (C) is not so   (D) have been

Q16. Timothy (   ) in the office at that time.

    (A) smoke   (B) was smoking   (C) had smoking   (D) will smoking

Strategy for Part 6 《長文穴埋め問題の解き方》

　　Part 6 は「長文穴埋め問題」ですので、Part 5 のように 1 つの文ではなく、複数の文で構成される文書となります。よって、時間がかかると考えてしまいがちです。しかし、設問をよく見ると、実は全て穴埋め問題です。Part 6 を、文書の意味をじっくり理解する「長文読解問題」とは考えずに、「Part 5 の『短文穴埋め問題』が、少しだけ長い文書の中に 4 問組み込まれている問題」と考えると良いでしょう。複数の文で構成されていますので、**空所のある文だけでなく、その前後の文を見ることも必要**となります。

　　Part 5 と Part 6 を手際よく解くことで、**Part 7 に使うことのできる時間をできるだけ増やすようにしましょう。**

▶ Part 6 Text Completion

次の英文を読んで、選択肢の中から空所に入る最も適切な語句を選びましょう。

Dear Mr. Schmitt,

I am writing to invite your company to participate in the Futaba City Tourism Exhibition this year. This is the tenth anniversary of the event, and this year we have by far the most companies and organizations ------- the event. ------- .
　　　　　　　　　　　　　　　　　　　　　　　　　　　　　　　　17.　　　　　**18.**

Furthermore, we are ------- to hear that many foreign travel companies are
　　　　　　　　　　19.
showing a great interest in the exhibition, especially this year. ------- the
　　　　　　　　　　　　　　　　　　　　　　　　　　　　　　20.
exhibition will not start until next month, we have already received many applications for booths from overseas. If you are planning to join us, we recommend sending an application online immediately because the number of booths is very limited.

Kind regards,

Ms. Takako Yoshida
Senior manager, the Tourism Bureau of Futaba City
tyoshida@tb-futaba.or.jp

Q17. (A) attended　　　(B) have attended　　(C) attending　　　(D) will attend

Q18. (A) As a result, we decided to hire less staff than last year.
　　　(B) In other words, the number of tourists is decreasing.
　　　(C) Likewise, there were no major changes to the budget.
　　　(D) Thus, the venue will be almost twice as large as last year.

Q19. (A) pleased　　　(B) sorry　　　　(C) afraid　　　(D) expected

Q20. (A) Although　　　(B) Instead of　　(C) Unless　　　(D) Provided that

Part 7 の全体像と時間配分

　リーディングセクション最後の Part 7 は「読解問題」で、本番では 54 の設問から成っています。文書については、最初の 29 問（本番では設問 147 〜設問 175）がシングル・パッセージで、10 問（本番では設問 176 〜設問 185）がダブル・パッセージ、15 問（本番では設問 186 〜設問 200）がトリプル・パッセージです。**Part 7 全体に、およそ 50 〜 55 分の時間を割けるよう、時間配分に注意し、自分なりのペースをつかんでおきましょう。**「1 分間に何語読むことができるか（wpm）」を定期的に計ることをお勧めします。

▶ Part 7 Single Passage

次の英文を読んで、設問に対する答えとして最も適切なものを選択肢の中から選びましょう。

To: Samantha Hall <Samantha.hall@g-wave.net>
From: Vincent Grace <vgrace@arrivatravel.com>
Date: April 30
Subject: Confirmation

Dear Ms. Hall:

Thank you very much for choosing Arriva Travel Ltd. for your vacation. This is to confirm your reservation for the tour. For the details, please find your travel itinerary attached. Now your full payment must be made no later than May 17. Please note that, if you cancel the reservation after May 23, an extra fee will be incurred. We will send you the airline ticket by e-mail after we have confirmed your payment.

Also, you will have some free time on Day 3 (June 21) and Day 5 (June 23) of the tour. We can offer you a variety of optional excursions on both of these days. Please see the other attachment to this e-mail for further information.

If you have any further inquiries, please do not hesitate to contact us.
Best regards,
Vincent Grace
Customer Manager
Arriva Travel Ltd.

Q21. What is the purpose of the e-mail?

(A) To cancel a reservation

(B) To apply for the optional events

(C) To confirm a booking

(D) To send a bill

Q22. When is the whole payment due?

(A) On April 30

(B) On May 17

(C) On May 23

(D) On June 23

Q23. What will Ms. Hall receive after her payment?

(A) An itinerary

(B) An application form

(C) A receipt

(D) An airline ticket

Q24. The word "incurred" in paragraph 1, line 5, is closest in meaning to

(A) charged

(B) paid

(C) returned

(D) deducted

Q25. What is suggested about the tour?

(A) It is popular among young people.

(B) Its price is affordable.

(C) Cancellation is not always free.

(D) It lasts for a week.

ボキャブラリーアルファ 1 Sightseeing / Guided Tour

この章のトピックでよく出る単語と表現です。日本語訳を見ながら英単語を声に出して言ってみましょう。

●観光 / ガイドのトピックに出てくる単語　🎵 1-16

1 ☐ **invite** [inváit]	動	招待する、依頼する、	
2 ☐ **weather** [wéðə(r)]	名	気候、天候	
3 ☐ **generation** [dʒènəréiʃən]	名	同世代の人々、世代	
4 ☐ **prevent** [privént]	動	妨げる、予防する	
5 ☐ **journey** [dʒə́:(r)ni]	名	旅行、旅程	
6 ☐ **spectacular** [spektǽkjələ(r)]	形	目を見張るほどの	
7 ☐ **reservation** [rèzə(r)véiʃən]	名	予約	
8 ☐ **refund** [rí:fʌnd]	名	払戻金	
9 ☐ **offshore** [ɔ́fʃɔ́:(r)]	形	沖合の、海外の	
10 ☐ **accommodation** [əkàmədéiʃən]	名	宿泊施設	
11 ☐ **feature** [fí:tʃə(r)]	名	特徴、特集記事	動 特集する
12 ☐ **waterfall** [wɔ́:tə(r)fɔ̀:l]	名	滝	
13 ☐ **tax** [tǽks]	名	税金、重い負担	
14 ☐ **spot** [spát]	名	場所、斑点、しみ	
15 ☐ **carpool** [kárpù:l]	名	車の相乗り	
16 ☐ **staff** [stǽf]	名	職員、スタッフ	
17 ☐ **ancient** [éinʃnt]	形	古代の、旧式の	
18 ☐ **photograph** [fóutəgræf]	名	写真	

●観光 / ガイドのトピックに出てくる表現　🎵 1-17

19 ☐ **fire extinguisher**	消火器
20 ☐ **lost and found**	遺失物取扱所
21 ☐ **summer retreat**	夏の避暑地
22 ☐ **vacation package**	休暇旅行プラン
23 ☐ **landmark building**	歴史的な建物
24 ☐ **night owl**	夜更かしする人
25 ☐ **courtesy car**	送迎車
26 ☐ **emergency exit**	非常口
27 ☐ **shuttle bus**	往復バス
28 ☐ **municipal bus**	市営バス
29 ☐ **prior approval**	事前承認
30 ☐ **scenic spots**	景勝地

UNIT 2 Restaurant

▶ Key Vocabulary 1-18

この章に出てくる下の英単語の中から日本語訳に当てはまる記号を（ ）に記入しましょう。
答え合わせをしたら音声を聞いて英単語を声に出して読み、つづりを書き込み覚えましょう。

●レストランのトピックに出てくる単語

1.	水をやる	（ ）	9.	頻繁に	（ ）
2.	前菜	（ ）	10.	委員会	（ ）
3.	単調な	（ ）	11.	地図	（ ）
4.	その代わり	（ ）	12.	暫定的な	（ ）
5.	見積もり	（ ）	13.	予定を立て直す	（ ）
6.	料理の	（ ）	14.	提案	（ ）
7.	移転させる	（ ）	15.	材料	（ ）
8.	コーディネーター	（ ）	16.	感謝	（ ）

a. frequently b. suggestion c. instead d. appetizer
e. relocate f. culinary g. tentative h. coordinator
i. reschedule j. map k. water l. appreciation
m. monotonous n. ingredient o. committee p. estimate

LISTENING SECTION

Strategy for Part 1 ≪写真描写問題の解き方≫

風景、室内の写真①　写真にあるものを確認しておこう
下の Warming-Up の写真を見ながら**日本語で描写してみましょう**。
●写真には**椅子**が写っている。　●写真には**人物**が写っていない。
●**窓**が見える。　●壁には**絵**がかかっている。　●天井から**照明**が吊るされている。

 Warming-Up 1-19

音声を聞いて（　　　）内の語を穴埋めし、
正しい答えはどれか選びましょう。

(A) （　　　　　　） are entering the restaurant.
(B) The （　　　　　） is being cleaned.
(C) There is a picture on the （　　　）.
(D) The （　　　） have been stacked in the
corner.　　　正しい答え　(A) (B) (C) (D)

▶ Part 1 Photographs

英文を聞き、4つの中から最も適切な描写を選びましょう。

Q1.

Ⓐ Ⓑ Ⓒ Ⓓ

Q2.

Ⓐ Ⓑ Ⓒ Ⓓ

Strategy for Part 2 ≪応答問題の解き方≫

疑問詞を聞き取ろう②　When で始まる疑問文

　疑問文が When で始まったら、まず頭の中で「いつ、いつ、いつ？」と繰り返しながら疑問詞の意味を記憶に残しておきます。「日時」や「時刻」を聞かれているので時制に注意して正解を選びましょう。

🔴 Warming-Up 🎵1-22

音声を聞いて、それぞれ、正しい応答の穴埋めをしましょう。

① **Q:** When will you eat your lunch?　**A:** In just a few (　　　　　　). ◎正解
② **Q:** When did he order the delivery pizza?　**A:** At (　　　　　　). ◎正解
　　↓以下のように直接時間を答えていないものでも正解になります。
③ **Q:** When does the restaurant open?　**A:** It hasn't been (　　　　　　)
　　　　　　　　　　　　　　　　　　　　　　yet. ◎正解

▶ Part 2 Question-Response

設問に対する応答として、最も適切なものを選びましょう。

Q3. Mark your answer on your answer sheet.　　Ⓐ Ⓑ Ⓒ
Q4. Mark your answer on your answer sheet.　　Ⓐ Ⓑ Ⓒ
Q5. Mark your answer on your answer sheet.　　Ⓐ Ⓑ Ⓒ
Q6. Mark your answer on your answer sheet.　　Ⓐ Ⓑ Ⓒ

Strategy for Part 3 ≪会話問題の解き方≫

2人の会話問題②　似ている選択肢が並ぶ時

　Part 3 の設問の先読みと同時に、**似ている選択肢が並ぶパターン**を攻略しておきましょう。

設問 At what time did the woman eat her breakfast?
- **(A)** At 9:00 a.m.
- **(B)** At 10:30 a.m.
- **(C)** At 11:00 a.m.
- **(D)** At 11:30 a.m.

設問を読まなくても選択肢を見ただけで時間が聞かれていることが明らかです。そしてさらに設問を読むことにより、聞くべきポイントの手掛かりをつかむことができます。

● Warming-Up

次の設問を読んで、会話の内容を予測しましょう。

　At what time did the woman eat her breakfast?
→女性が（　　　　　　）を食べた時間が問われていて、その時間は必ず選択肢の中のどれかであるとわかる。

▶ Part 3 Short Conversation

 1-27,28

会話文を聞いて、各設問に対する最も適切な答えを4つの選択肢から選びましょう。

Q7. Where does the man most likely work?
- (A) At an employment agency
- (B) At a trading company
- (C) At a catering company
- (D) At a bookstore

Q8. According to the woman, approximately how many people are coming for the anniversary event?
- (A) 10 people
- (B) 15 people
- (C) 20 people
- (D) 60 people

Q9. What will the man probably do next?
- (A) Visit the restaurant
- (B) Fix some sandwiches
- (C) Read a proposal
- (D) Provide an estimate

トークの「展開」はほぼ決まっている！①

　皆さんは Part 4 のトークにどんな印象を持っていますか。「捉えどころがない」でしょうか。実は、多くのトークを比較してみると、**同じ種類のトークでは、その展開もだいたい同じ**で、受験者の意表を突くような展開をするトークはほとんどないのです。練習では、常に**トークの「筋書き」を意識**しましょう。

⏺ Warming-Up 🎧1-29

次の、説明文（トーク）に入る前に流れる音声を、スクリプトを見ながら聞きましょう。トークの種類は何でしょうか。正しいものを１つ選び、○で囲みましょう。
「音声スクリプト」"Questions 10 through 12 refer to the following announcement."
（答え：会議の一部・留守電メッセージ・広告・人物紹介・公共放送・アナウンス）

▶ Part 4 Short Talk

説明文を聞いて、各設問に対する最も適切な答えを４つの選択肢から選びましょう。

Q10. What happened at Ciao Bella Kitchen last week?

(A) It hired some new staff.

(B) It was relocated.

(C) It held a contest.

(D) It was reopened.

Q11. Who is Paul Jordan?

(A) A professional cook

(B) A local farmer

(C) A business owner

(D) An event coordinator

Q12. What will be available on the Web site soon?

(A) A new location map

(B) A list of the award-winners

(C) Some photographs

(D) Some recipes

READING SECTION

Strategy for Part 5 ≪短文穴埋め問題のための Grammar ≫

動詞の形問題② 「人称」と「単数」か「複数」か、を考えよう

　前のユニットでは、**まず「主語」と「動詞」を探すこと**。そして、**空所に述語動詞が入るとわかったら、主語の人称と、単数か、複数か、また「時制」について考えること**に触れました。ではこの章では主語の「人称」と「単複」をみていきましょう。

　主格の主語の人称にはI/we の1人称（話し手）、you の2人称（相手）、he/she/it/they などの3人称（第三者）があります。そして I は単数、we は複数のように、**単数、複数に区別**できます。

ここで、**所有格**（＝直後の名詞にかかる）、**目的格**（＝動詞の目的語になる、前置詞の後に続けられる）も確認しておきましょう。

	1人称単数	2人称単数	3人称単数		
主　　　格	I	you	he	she	it
所　有　格	my	your	his	her	its
目　的　格	me	you	him	her	it
所有代名詞	mine	yours	his	hers	
再帰代名詞	myself	yourself	himself	herself	itself

	1人称複数	2人称複数	3人称複数
主　　　格	we	you	they
所　有　格	our	your	their
目　的　格	us	you	them
所有代名詞	ours	yours	theirs
再帰代名詞	ourselves	yourselves	themselves

また、**所有代名詞は「所有格＋名詞」の役割を果たし、再帰代名詞は「〜自身」**の意味で、主語と重複する目的語に使ったり、強調したりするのに用います。

Warming-Up

次の英文の主語の人称、単複に注目し、続く動詞を選び、正しい方を○で囲みましょう。

(1) I (have · has) a pain in my stomach.

(2) She (tend · tends) to be emotional when she is hungry.

(3) I (hate · hates) to admit it, but you are a good cook.

(4) Cellular phones (is · are) useful for making reservations.

(5) Our company (sells · sell) a variety of cooking utensils.

(6) You (have · has) the potential to become a food journalist.

▶ Part 5 Incomplete Sentences

空所に入る最も適切な語句を選びましょう。

Q13. Jennifer (   ) five evenings a week at the diner nearby.

    (A) work   (B) works   (C) have worked   (D) had worked

Q14. Although I had my portable music player serviced, it still turns off by (   ).

    (A) themselves   (B) itself   (C) its   (D) their

Q15. The people in this building frequently (   ) Chinese lunch boxes from next door.

    (A) order   (B) orders   (C) ordering   (D) will order

Q16. Jackson Furniture's summer party (   ) next Wednesday in the cafeteria.

    (A) holds   (B) will be held   (C) to hold   (D) was held

Strategy for Part 6 ≪長文穴埋め問題の解き方≫

　Part 6 では、始めに文書全体を一気に読み通し、次に選択肢を見てから一気に解答しましょう。また、TOEIC は 2016 年 5 月に新形式となり、Part 6 では空欄に入る「文」を選ぶ問題が出題されるようになりました。このいわゆる「文選択問題」が加わったことでそれまで以上に**「文書の文脈（ストーリー）を読み取る」**ことが重視されるようになりました。文脈を読み取るためには、文書を一通りさっと読むこと（スキミング skimming）が必要です。また以上より、**文選択問題は、4 問の最後に解く**ことをお勧めめします。

▶ Part 6 Text Completion

次の英文を読んで、選択肢の中から空所に入る最も適切な語句を選びましょう。

To: Alice McLaren
From: Peter Wu
Date: July 31
Subject: Best Chef in Gatwick Awards 2018

Dear Ms. McLaren,

We are delighted to inform you that the Gatwick Culinary Contest committee has decided to give you this year's Best Chef in Gatwick Award. Congratulations!

------. However, we would like you to attend the awards ceremony too, which
17.
------- in the city hall on the 20th of August. This is not only for giving you the
18.
award but also introducing you as a successful local resident to the public. We would appreciate it if you could share some of your ------- time with the people
19.
of Gatwick city.
We are, for example, hoping you could hold one of ------- cooking and talk
20.
sessions with local residents on the stage after the ceremony.

We look forward to hearing from you soon.

Sincerely,
Peter Wu
Regional Promotion Manager
Gatwick Municipal Office

Q17. (A) We understand that you are busy with your restaurant.
(B) It is nice to hear that you are doing good business.
(C) This award is well-known all over the country.
(D) The schedule has not yet been decided.

Q18. (A) holds   (B) has been held   (C) is holding   (D) will be held

Q19. (A) wasteful   (B) abandon   (C) precious   (D) boring

Q20. (A) you   (B) your   (C) yours   (D) yourself

設問の種類

　Part 7 の設問には**いくつかの決まった種類があります**。テスト本番で効率的に設問を読むために、あらかじめそれぞれの設問の種類を分類し、各種類の設問の特徴、またそれぞれ正解を導くためには文書のどこを見ればよいか、などを理解しておきましょう。

1. 全体の内容を問うパターン　　　　　**2.** 個別の詳細を問うパターン

3. 書き手の意図を推測するパターン　　**4.** 単語の意味を問うパターン

5. 文が入る位置を問うパターン

▶ Part 7 Single Passage

次の英文を読んで、設問に対する答えとして最も適切なものを選択肢の中から選びましょう。

---

17 August

Dear Mr. Russell,

I am writing in response to your invitation to the cooking seminar for local culinary school students. - [1] -. I am glad to have the chance to work with these future chefs and it would be my pleasure to attend the event as a guest speaker.

However, having seen the tentative schedule for the seminar, I am afraid to tell you that I will be out of town from the 29th to the 31st of August. - [2] -. Therefore, I was wondering if you could reschedule the seminar for the following month so that I can attend.

- [3] -. As for the seminar, cooking with the students sounds very interesting to me, and I would also like to make a few suggestions. - [4] -. I believe that will get them more involved in the event. Also, why don't we use as many locally grown ingredients as we can? I hope this will make the students more aware of the importance of the fishing industry in our town.

Thank you very much again for inviting me to this wonderful event.

Sincerely,
Daniel Hashimoto
Chief Chef
Japanese Restaurant Kagetsu

Q21. Why is Mr. Hashimoto writing to Mr. Russell?

(A) To inform him of his absence
(B) To invite him to the seminar
(C) To show his appreciation
(D) To request him to change the venue

Q22. What is indicated about the seminar?

(A) Its schedule has been fixed.
(B) Some students will take part in it.
(C) It will be held at the school.
(D) Some lectures will be provided.

Q23. What is suggested about Mr. Hashimoto?

(A) He will retire next month.
(B) He graduated from a local school.
(C) He will be taking a vacation.
(D) He is very interested in the event.

Q24. What does Mr. Hashimoto suggest doing for the event?

(A) Advertising the event in the paper
(B) Asking local companies for donations
(C) Using food grown nearby
(D) Inviting the local residents

Q25. In which of the positions marked [1], [2], [3], and [4] does the following sentence best belong?

"First of all, it would be good if the students decided the menu themselves."

(A) [1]   (B) [2]   (C) [3]   (D) [4]

▶ ボキャブラリーアルファ 2 Restaurant

この章のトピックでよく出る単語と表現です。日本語訳を見ながら英単語を声に出して言ってみましょう。

●レストランのトピックに出てくる単語　🎵 1-32

1 ☐ **favorite** [féiv(ə)rət]	形	お気に入りの	
2 ☐ **wine** [wáin]	名	ワイン、果実酒	
3 ☐ **smell** [smél]	名	におい	動 におう
4 ☐ **smoke** [smóuk]	名	煙、喫煙	
5 ☐ **dish** [díʃ]	名	皿、料理	
6 ☐ **fruit** [frúːt]	名	果物、成果	
7 ☐ **attract** [ətrǽkt]	動	引き付ける、魅了する	
8 ☐ **leftover** [léftòuvə(r)]	名	食べ残し	
9 ☐ **bowl** [bóul]	名	椀、椀一杯分の料理	
10 ☐ **refreshment** [rifréʃmənt]	名	軽い食事、飲食物	
11 ☐ **vicinity** [visínəti]	名	近所、周辺	
12 ☐ **original** [ərídʒənl]	形	最初の	
13 ☐ **sour** [sáuə(r)]	形	酸っぱい、いじわるな	
14 ☐ **cuisine** [kwizíːn]	名	独特の料理	
15 ☐ **wheat** [(h)wíːt]	名	小麦	
16 ☐ **fat** [fǽt]	名	脂肪、料理用の脂	
17 ☐ **vine** [váin]	名	ブドウの木	
18 ☐ **atmosphere** [ǽtməsfiə(r)]	名	大気、雰囲気	

●レストランのトピックに出てくる表現　🎵 1-33

19 ☐ **frozen food**	冷凍食品
20 ☐ **expiration date**	賞味期限
21 ☐ **Chinese restaurant**	中華料理店
22 ☐ **fast-food restaurant**	ファーストフード店
23 ☐ **freshly baked pie**	焼きたてのパイ
24 ☐ **home delivery**	宅配
25 ☐ **grilled beef**	牛肉のあぶり焼き
26 ☐ **vintage wine**	年代物のワイン
27 ☐ **seasonal delicacy**	季節のご馳走
28 ☐ **a slice of bread**	パン一枚
29 ☐ **culinary art**	料理法、調理法
30 ☐ **dairy product**	乳製品

UNIT 3 Hotel / Service

▶ Key Vocabulary

 1-34

この章に出てくる下の英単語の中から日本語訳に当てはまる記号を（　）に記入しましょう。
答え合わせをしたら音声を聞いて英単語を声に出して読み、つづりを書き込み覚えましょう。

● ホテル / サービスのトピックに出てくる単語

1.	傷口	（　）	9.	予想する	（　）
2.	休日	（　）	10.	禁止	（　）
3.	定期購読する	（　）	11.	罰金を科す	（　）
4.	予約する	（　）	12.	破る	（　）
5.	予算	（　）	13.	苦情	（　）
6.	見積もり	（　）	14.	規制	（　）
7.	愛顧	（　）	15.	感謝	（　）
8.	アンケート	（　）	16.	保護者	（　）

a. estimate	**b.** complaint	**c.** questionnaire	**d.** subscribe
e. gratitude	**f.** day off	**g.** guardian	**h.** fine
i. predict	**j.** ban	**k.** patronage	**l.** wound
m. book	**n.** violate	**o.** regulation	**p.** budget

LISTENING SECTION

Strategy for Part 1 ≪写真描写問題の解き方≫

人物の写真②　人物の動きに注目しよう

下の Warming-Up の写真を見ながら男性が何をしているか考えましょう。

● 人物が一人だけ写っている写真、もしくは複数の人物が写っていて、一人の人物が目立っている場合は、選択肢の主語が全部同じ語で統一されていることが多いです。この場合、難易度は高くないので、人物の動作を表す動詞に集中しましょう。

Warming-Up 1-35

音声を聞いて (　　　) 内に動詞を〜 ing の形にして穴埋めし、正しい答えはどれか選びましょう。

(A) He's (　　　　　　　) the desk.
(B) He's (　　　　　　　) his teeth.
(C) He's (　　　　　　　) on the telephone.
(D) He's (　　　　　　　) on his tie.

正しい答え　(A) (B) (C) (D)

英文を聞き、4つの中から最も適切な描写を選びましょう。

Q1.

Ⓐ Ⓑ Ⓒ Ⓓ

Q2.

Ⓐ Ⓑ Ⓒ Ⓓ

Strategy for Part 2 ≪応答問題の解き方≫

疑問詞を聞き取ろう③　Why で始まる疑問文

　Whyで始まる疑問文は基本的には「理由」を聞いています。Part 2では疑問詞で始まる設問に対して、"Yes" や "No" で始まる選択肢はほぼ不正解です。Whyに対して単純にBecauseで始まる選択肢も誤答を誘っている場合が多いので気を付けましょう。

● Warming-Up 🎧1-38

音声を聞いて、疑問文とその答えの意味を記入しましょう。

　Q: Why did she decide to go to Spain?　(　　　　　　　　　　　)

　A: She just wanted to visit her friends.　(　　　　　　　　　　　)

► **Part 2 Question-Response**

設問に対する応答として、最も適切なものを選びましょう。

Q3. Mark your answer on your answer sheet.　　Ⓐ Ⓑ Ⓒ

Q4. Mark your answer on your answer sheet.　　Ⓐ Ⓑ Ⓒ

Q5. Mark your answer on your answer sheet.　　Ⓐ Ⓑ Ⓒ

Q6. Mark your answer on your answer sheet.　　Ⓐ Ⓑ Ⓒ

Strategy for Part 3 《会話問題の解き方》

図表を含む問題①　図表を見て、何のテーマか考えよう

　図表を含む問題では音声が流れる前に設問と図表を見ておく必要があります。しかし図表を見ただけで正解できてしまってはリスニングの問題とならないので、音声と図表の内容の両方から正解を導き出すようになっています。

⚪ Warming-Up

下の Part 3 の問題の図表を見て、図表の左と右に何が書いてあるのか答えましょう。

　左側（ホテルの ＿＿＿＿＿＿＿＿＿＿＿＿＿＿＿＿＿＿＿ が書いてある。）

　右側（会議室の ＿＿＿＿＿＿＿＿＿＿＿＿＿＿＿＿＿＿＿ が書いてある。）

▶ Part 3　Short Conversation

 1-43,44

会話文を聞いて、各設問に対する最も適切な答えを 4 つの選択肢から選びましょう。

Hotel's Name	Rental Price for conference rooms
Lloyd Hotel	$260.00
Princess Hotel	$350.00
Miami Hotel	$600.00　includes a buffet
Crystal Hotel	$980.00　includes a buffet

Q7. What type of event are the speakers discussing?

(A) An award ceremony　　　　　(B) A reception event

(C) A store's opening　　　　　(D) A retirement party

Q8. What is the woman considering?

(A) When to schedule the event　(B) Which hotel to choose

(C) Whose estimate is correct　　(D) How to hire new employees

Q9. Look at the graphic. Which hotel will they probably choose?

(A) Lloyd Hotel　　　　　　　(B) Princess Hotel

(C) Miami Hotel　　　　　　　(D) Crystal Hotel

トークの「展開」はほぼ決まっている！②

Part 4 に登場するトークに、「**公共放送 (broadcast, radio broadcast, news broadcast)**」があります。ラジオ放送などにおいて、聞き手は誰でしょうか…そう、不特定多数の人々ですね。そして、そこでよく取り上げられているトピックには、一体どんなものが多いのでしょうか。

🔵 Warming-Up 🎧 1-45

次の、説明文（トーク）に入る前に流れる音声を、スクリプトを見ながら聞きましょう。
「音声スクリプト」"Questions 10 through 12 refer to the following radio broadcast"
この音声が聞こえた場合、よく取り上げられるトーク内容を4つ選び、〇で囲みましょう。
（答え：天気予報・交通情報・留守電応答メッセージ・ビジネスニュース・イベント情報）

▶ Part 4 Short Talk

 1-46,47

説明文を聞いて、各設問に対する最も適切な答えを4つの選択肢から選びましょう。

Q10. What type of business is Greenwich Ocean?

    (A) A music band

    (B) A travel agency

    (C) An event planning company

    (D) A local hotel

Q11. When was the business opened?

    (A) 2 years ago

    (B) 10 years ago

    (C) 20 years ago

    (D) 50 years ago

Q12. How can the listeners join the event?

    (A) By booking a room online

    (B) By answering a survey

    (C) By visiting a ticket office

    (D) By applying for membership

READING SECTION

Strategy for Part 5　≪短文穴埋め問題のための Grammar ≫

動詞の形問題③　「現在形」か「現在進行形」か。「過去形」か「現在完了形」か。

　Unit 1 では主語と動詞の「時制」について考えることに触れました。まず選択肢をみて、「動詞の形」の問題だと判断できたら、**時制を考える際の「現在形」と「現在進行形」の見極めと、「過去形」と「現在完了形」の違いを明確にしましょう。時を表す修飾語句は大きなヒントになります。**

☆「現在形」か「現在進行形」か
　「現在形」は現在の状況を表します、**「現在進行形」は《be 動詞 + 現在分詞》の形で、「現在進行中の動作、出来事」「現在の反復的な動作」**を表します。

💡**ヒント**　時を表す修飾語句　・now（今は）currently（現在は）など

☆「過去形」か「現在完了形」か
　「過去形」は現在から切り離された過去について、「現在完了形」は《have(has)＋ 過去分詞》の形で、現在とつながりのある過去を表します。

・過去の一時期の状況・出来事を表す「～した」→「過去形」
Kate went to the swimming pool last week.
（ケイトは先週プールに行きました。）

💡**ヒント**　時を表す修飾語句　・yesterday（昨日は）last week（先週は）
　　　　　　 ten years ago（10 年前は）when she was born（彼女が生まれた時に）
　　　　　　 in 1960（1960 年に）など

・動作の完了、その結果としての現在の状態を表す「～してしまった」→「現在完了形」
The professor has gone to Chicago on business.
（その教授は仕事でシカゴに行ってしまいました。）

・現在までの経験、継続を表す「～したことがある」「ずっと～している」→「現在完了形」
They've been married for 20 years.
（彼らは結婚してから 20 年になります。）

💡**ヒント**　時を表す修飾語句　・for ten years（10 年間）　since 2014（2014 年から）
　　　　　　 など

Warming-Up

次の時を表す修飾語句が表す時制を選んで正しい方を○で囲みましょう。

    (1) since last week   (過去形 ・ 現在完了形)
    (2) when I was in school   (過去形 ・ 現在完了形)
    (3) in 1980   (過去形 ・ 現在完了形)
    (4) for the past 3 months   (過去形 ・ 現在完了形)

▶ Part 5 Incomplete Sentences

空所に入る最も適切な語句を選びましょう。

Q13. I (   ) the problem with the oven before the chef arrived.
    (A) will solve   (B) solve   (C) have solved   (D) had solved

Q14. The chef (   ) that the diner would enjoy the shrimp.
    (A) prediction   (B) predicted   (C) predicting   (D) predicts

Q15. The automatic door is undergoing maintenance and (   ) shut down since Friday evening.
    (A) will   (B) had   (C) has been   (D) will be

Q16. Max Hamburger (   ) over 20 shops across Canada by next year.
    (A) will have   (B) will be   (C) have   (D) has had

Strategy for Part 6 ≪長文穴埋め問題の解き方≫

　　Part 6に登場する文書の単語数は大体100語前後ですので、それほど長くはありません。しかもその種類は非常に限られています。その中の一つが「**掲示 (notice)**」です。ここで、掲示とはどのような時に出されるものか、考えてみましょう。多くは「不特定多数の人々に、何かを特別に知らせたい」時ですね。そのような視点で、文書のストーリー（文脈）を追ってみてはいかがでしょうか。

▶ Part 6 Text Completion

次の英文を読んで、選択肢の中から空所に入る最も適切な語句を選びましょう。

> Thank you for staying at the Sunrise Hotel. Earlier this year, the town ------- a
> 17.
> total smoking ban in public buildings, including hotels. For all of our valued
> guests to have a comfortable stay, we would like to ask you not to smoke
> anywhere in this hotel. -------. For example, anyone found smoking will be fined
> 18.
> up to $1,000 for violating the ban. Since there were many complaints about
> passive smoking from non-smokers at the hotel, we set up a smoking room on
> the first floor five years ago. -------, following the new regulation, the room is no
> 19.
> longer available. For smokers, please use the ------- smoking area behind the
> 20.
> building.

Q17. (A) introduced   (B) is introduced

      (C) will introduce   (D) has been introduced

Q18. (A) The regulations are very strict.

      (B) Smoking is not good for your health.

      (C) The rule is not applied to all of the guests.

      (D) The reception has been moved upstairs.

Q19. (A) However   (B) Moreover

      (C) Besides   (D) Alternatively

Q20. (A) designated   (B) distributed

      (C) distant   (D) determined

Strategy for Part 7 《読解問題の解き方》

設問パターン①

　Unit 2 で紹介した Part 7 の設問の種類のうちの、「**1. 全体の内容を問うパターン**」は、「文書の中の情報をもとに推測する問題」とも言えます。

　2016 年の「新形式」への変更以来、TOEIC L&R のリーディングは「**受験者に文書をしっかり読ませる**」ための**出題傾向**が強くなりました。皆さんは Part 7 を解く際、文書と設問の間を頻繁に行ったり来たりしていませんか。これで解ける問題もあることは事実ですが、反面、この解き方で時間を無駄にすることも多いのです。

　「**まずは一通り、文書を全部読む**」…少なくとも練習の際は、これを心がけてみてはいかがでしょうか。どこに何が書いてあるか、よりよく見えるようになれば、このパターンの問題がより多く解けるようになるはずです。

次の英文を読んで、設問に対する答えとして最も適切なものを選択肢の中から選びましょう。

To: Atunima Jonathan <atunimajonathan@mk-pharmacy.com>
From: Patricia May <pmay@cphotel.com>
Date: July 7
Subject: Summer events in 2021

Dear Mr. Jonathan,

Thank you for answering our customer survey online. As a token of our gratitude for your continued patronage, we would like to invite you to attend our fifth anniversary event which takes place next month. The details are as follows:

Monday, August 5
We are inviting up to 50 people to a music concert at the banquet hall. Gatwick Orchestra will take you to the wonderland of classical music. Children aged under 6 are not allowed to enter. Have a good evening and enjoy the lovely music! - [1] -.

Wednesday, August 7
Now that the renovation of the outdoor swimming pool has been completed, it will be open to up to 30 children and their guardians from 10 a.m. to 4 p.m. There will be a new exciting water slide. Why don't you enjoy it with your children?
 - [2] -.

Friday, August 9
Celebrating the final day of our event week, Shane Brighton, our chief chef, will be offering you a special dinner. He has already created a fabulous menu for it. - [3] -.

If you are interested in any event mentioned above, please log-in to our Web site to apply and use the promotional code "cphotel2021." Please note that you can apply for one event only, and we will send out invitations on a first-come-first-served basis. - [4] -.

We look forward to welcoming you again soon.

Sincerely,
Patricia May, Promotion Manager, City Plaza Hotel

Q21. What is suggested about Atunima Jonathan?
    (A) He will be attending an event.
    (B) He conducted a survey.
    (C) He will be taking a vacation.
    (D) He has stayed at this hotel before.

Q22. What is the purpose of the e-mail?
    (A) To advertise a discount
    (B) To accept an invitation
    (C) To show appreciation
    (D) To answer a questionnaire

Q23. What is true about the hotel?
    (A) It was opened five years ago.
    (B) It holds some events every summer.
    (C) It will be renovated next month.
    (D) It has been highly evaluated.

Q24. The word "fabulous" in paragraph 4, line 3, is closest in meaning to
    (A) superb   (B) tasty   (C) various   (D) affordable

Q25. In which of the positions marked [1], [2], [3], and [4] does the following sentence best belong?
    "Please remember, the number of seats is limited to 70."
    (A) [1]   (B) [2]   (C) [3]   (D) [4]

▶ ボキャブラリーアルファ 3 Hotel / Service

この章のトピックでよく出る単語と表現です。日本語訳を見ながら英単語を声に出して言ってみましょう。

●ホテル / サービスのトピックに出てくる単語 🎧 1-48

1 ☐ **illuminate** [ilúːmənèit]	動	照らす、明らかにする
2 ☐ **identify** [aidéntəfài]	動	識別する、確認する
3 ☐ **limit** [límit]	動	制限する
4 ☐ **restore** [ristɔ́ː(r)]	動	回復させる
5 ☐ **complimentary** [kàmpləmént(ə)ri]	形	無料の
6 ☐ **rate** [réit]	名	割合、率
7 ☐ **advertisement** [ǽdvə(r)táizmənt]	名	広告
8 ☐ **beverage** [bév(ə)ridʒ]	名	飲み物、飲料
9 ☐ **flavor** [fléivə(r)]	名	風味
10 ☐ **emphasize** [émfəsàiz]	動	強調する
11 ☐ **housekeeper** [háuskìːpə(r)]	名	ハウスキーパー、家政婦
12 ☐ **reception** [risépʃən]	名	晩さん会、レセプション
13 ☐ **notify** [nóutəfài]	動	通知する
14 ☐ **guide** [gáid]	名	ガイド、ガイド役
15 ☐ **complete** [kəmplíːt]	動	完結する、仕上げる
16 ☐ **positive** [pázətiv]	形	好意的な
17 ☐ **divide** [diváid]	動	分ける
18 ☐ **constantly** [kánst(ə)ntli]	副	常に
19 ☐ **patron** [péitr(ə)n]	名	後援者
20 ☐ **exclusive** [iksklúːsiv]	形	独占的な

●ホテル / サービスのトピックに出てくる表現 🎧 1-49

21 ☐ **check in**	記帳する、チェックインする
22 ☐ **local specialty**	地方の名産
23 ☐ **culinary implements**	台所用具
24 ☐ **hot spring resort**	温泉場
25 ☐ **customer satisfaction**	顧客満足
26 ☐ **hotel annex**	ホテルの別館
27 ☐ **front desk clerk**	フロント係
28 ☐ **breakfast special**	モーニングサービス
29 ☐ **high season**	観光客の多い時期
30 ☐ **sign language**	手話

▶ Key Vocabulary 1-50

この章に出てくる下の英単語の中から日本語訳に当てはまる記号を（　）に記入しましょう。
答え合わせをしたら音声を聞いて英単語を声に出して読み、つづりを書き込み覚えましょう。

●雇用のトピックに出てくる単語

1.	配布する	（　　）	9.	正確な	（　　）
2.	履歴書	（　　）	10.	内部で	（　　）
3.	志願者	（　　）	11.	合併する	（　　）
4.	参加者	（　　）	12.	撤退する	（　　）
5.	薬剤師	（　　）	13.	都合の悪い	（　　）
6.	証明書	（　　）	14.	決定する	（　　）
7.	手続き	（　　）	15.	子会社	（　　）
8.	議題	（　　）	16.	適用可能な	（　　）

a. participant **b.** withdraw **c.** certificate **d.** precise

e. determine **f.** applicable **g.** distribute **h.** subsidiary

i. internally **j.** pharmacist **k.** inconvenient **l.** agenda

m. procedure **n.** résumé **o.** merge **p.** applicant

LISTENING SECTION

Strategy for Part 1 ≪写真描写問題の解き方≫

写真にないものは間違い

下の Warming-Up の写真に出てくるものと、出てこないものを聞き分けましょう。

● 写真にないものが音声で聞こえてきたら、その選択肢は間違いです。選択肢の中で聞こえる音が写真にあるものを表しているかどうか、瞬時に判断しましょう。

 Warming-Up 1-51

音声を聞いて (　　　) 内の語を穴埋めし、
正しい答えはどれか選びましょう。

(A) (　　　　　　) are shaking hands.
(B) The (　　　　　　) are being repaired.
(C) There are some (　　　　　　　) on the wall.
(D) They are sitting on the (　　　　　　).

正しい答え　(A) (B) (C) (D)

31

▶ Part 1 Photographs

英文を聞き、4つの中から最も適切な描写を選びましょう。

Q1.

Ⓐ Ⓑ Ⓒ Ⓓ

Q2.

Ⓐ Ⓑ Ⓒ Ⓓ

....

Strategy for Part 2 《応答問題の解き方》

疑問詞を聞き取ろう④　Where で始まる疑問文

　Where で始まる疑問文は意味的に When と勘違いしないように注意しましょう。
Where で始まり「場所」を聞かれているのに時間を答えているものは間違いです。また、
例えば「居場所」など、広い場所を聞かれているのに「保管場所」のように狭い場所を答
えるのもよくある誤答選択肢です。設問に対して適切な応答を選びましょう。

Warming-Up 🔊 1-54

音声を聞いて、質問に対し、それぞれの応答が正しいかどうか○か×を記入しましょう。

　Q: Where have you been?　**(A)** In the drawer　　（　　）

　　　　　　　　　　　　　　(B) In three minutes　（　　）

　　　　　　　　　　　　　　(C) At the station　　（　　）

▶ Part 2 Question-Response

 1-55,56,57,58

設問に対する応答として、最も適切なものを選びましょう。

Q3. Mark your answer on your answer sheet.　　Ⓐ Ⓑ Ⓒ

Q4. Mark your answer on your answer sheet.　　Ⓐ Ⓑ Ⓒ

Q5. Mark your answer on your answer sheet.　　Ⓐ Ⓑ Ⓒ

Q6. Mark your answer on your answer sheet.　　Ⓐ Ⓑ Ⓒ

Strategy for Part 3 ≪会話問題の解き方≫

3人の会話問題①　同性の発言を聞き分ける

　設問を先読みし、"man"、"woman" の複数形、**"men"**、**"women"** が出てきたら、**3人の会話問題**であることが分かります。2人の会話では男女、3人の会話では男性2人女性1人または男性1人女性2人が登場します。複数いる人物を確認するつもりで心の準備をしてからリスニングに集中しましょう。

　会話の内容から男性2人、または女性2人の関係性や3人の関係性を理解しながら聞き進めます。

例えば、設問に

What do **the men** imply about the applicant?

とあったら、**女性は1人、男性が複数（2人）**いて、志願者に関する話をしていることが音声を聞く前にわかります。

Warming-Up

次の設問を読んで、会話の内容を予測しましょう。

Where did the women go yesterday?

→会話には**男性が**（　　　　　　　　　　　　）、**女性が複数（2人）**出てきて、女性達
　　が昨日、どこかに（　　　　　　　　　　　）ことがわかる。

▶ Part 3 Short Conversation

 1-59,60

会話文を聞いて、各設問に対する最も適切な答えを4つの選択肢から選びましょう。

Q7. Where most likely do the men work?

(A) At an employment agency

(B) At a trading company

(C) At a pharmacy

(D) At a bookstore

Q8. What happened to the woman last year?

(A) She suffered from a bad back injury.

(B) She became a doctor.

(C) She became addicted to alcohol.

(D) She met a boxer.

Q9. What will the men do for the woman?

(A) Offer her treatment

(B) Ask for counseling

(C) Hire her

(D) Provide her with music therapy

トークの「展開」はほぼ決まっている！③

　Part 4 によく登場するトークに、「**会議の一部（excerpt from a meeting）**」があります。では、会社などで行われる会議において、内容が比較的易しく、部外者（TOEIC 受験者）が聞いても理解できそうな部分はどこでしょう…一般的な連絡事項などの多い、**会議の「始め」**と**「終わり」**ではないでしょうか。また、そこでよく取り上げられる話題には、どんなものが多いのでしょうか。

🔵 Warming-Up 💿1-61

次の、説明文（トーク）に入る前の音声を、スクリプトを見ながら聞きましょう。
「音声スクリプト」"Questions 10 through 12 refer to the following excerpt from a meeting"
この音声が聞こえた場合、トークとして取り上げられることが比較的多いのは、会議のどの部分でしょうか。正しいものを 2 つ選び、○で囲みましょう。
（答え：会議開始直後の部分・会議の半ば頃・会議終了直前の部分）

▶ Part 4　Short Talk

 1-62,63

説明文を聞いて、各設問に対する最も適切な答えを 4 つの選択肢から選びましょう。

Q10. Which department does the speaker work in?
(A) Marketing
(B) Sales
(C) General affairs
(D) Accounting

Q11. What did the management decide to do yesterday?
(A) To hire some experts
(B) To raise a product price
(C) To merge with another company
(D) To withdraw from the market

Q12. What are the listeners asked to do if they know the right person for the job?
(A) Submit a report
(B) Apply for the positions
(C) Stay in the room
(D) Contact a coworker

READING SECTION

Strategy for Part 5 ≪短文穴埋め問題のための Grammar ≫

動詞の形問題④ 「自動詞」と「他動詞」を使い分けよう

☆「自動詞」って何？

「自動詞」は目的語を必要としない動詞です。つまり**直後に名詞を置くことができません。**

例えば、自動詞の return は「戻る」「帰る」の意味です。

目的語を置きたい場合、

　× The student returned school.

は間違いで、

　◎ The student returned to the school.

のように、動詞の後ろに前置詞が必要になります。

　※自動詞は目的語をとらないので受動態にはなりません。

☆「他動詞」って何？

「他動詞」は目的語を必要とする動詞です。**直後に目的語となる名詞などが続きます。**

例えば、他動詞 marry（～と結婚する）の目的語は「結婚する相手」です。

「ケントはクリスティーナと結婚する」は、

　◎ Kent will marry Christina. です。

　× Kent will marry. のように、目的語なしで使うことはできません。

また、日本語の感覚で（～と結婚する）

　× Kent will marry with Christina.

のように、前置詞を入れることはできません。

The campus relocation will (　　　　　) tomorrow.

　(A) be announced

　(B) announce

　(C) announced

　(D) announcing

上の問題では announce は「他動詞」。主語は The campus relocation「キャンパスの移転」なので、「人」ではなくて、「もの」が主語となっています。「もの」は自ら「発表する」わけではないので、「発表される」の受動態の形にします。(A) を正解に選びます。

参考訳）キャンパスの移転は明日発表されます。

⏺ Warming-Up

自動詞は目的語を取らないので受動態になりません。次の自動詞の意味を記入して受動態にならないことを確認してから覚えましょう。

(1) arrive　　(　　　　　　　　　　　　　　　　　)
(2) appear　 (　　　　　　　　　　　　　　　　　)
(3) occur　　(　　　　　　　　　　　　　　　　　)
(4) happen　 (　　　　　　　　　　　　　　　　　)
(5) exist　　 (　　　　　　　　　　　　　　　　　)

▶ Part 5 Incomplete Sentences

空所に入る最も適切な語句を選びましょう。

Q13. The managers will meet on Monday to (　　　) the next interview procedure.

(A) talk　　　　(B) talk about　　　　(C) tell　　　　(D) tell about

Q14. Training courses at the company (　　　) to long-term employees.

(A) offer　　　　(B) are offered　　　　(C) offering　　　　(D) have offered

Q15. It appears (　　　) a bit too soon to raise his salary.

(A) to be　　　　(B) like　　　　(C) that　　　　(D) to do

Q16. The signed contract (　　　) five days before the deadline.

(A) receive　　　　(B) will receive　　　　(C) received　　　　(D) was received

Strategy for Part 6 《長文穴埋め問題の解き方》

　Part 6 によく登場する文書の種類の一つに、「**手紙 (letter)**」があります。特に TOEIC L&R で出題される手紙は、友人などに宛てた個人的なものではなく、主に仕事上、何か伝える必要性のある内容を受取人へ知らせるものです。そこで、おのずと書き方も決まってきます。

　典型的なパターンとして、まずは「**手紙の目的**」、次に「**詳細**」、そして最後には「～してください」というような「**依頼**」が来ることが多いです。そのように考えれば、手紙 (letter) はとても読みやすい文書かもしれません。

▶ Part 6 Text Completion

次の英文を読んで、選択肢の中から空所に入る最も適切な語句を選びましょう。

Dear Ms. Emerson,

Thank you for applying for the position of chief sales representative. We're very impressed with the wonderful achievements in your résumé and would like to ------- an interview with you.
17.

-------. However, since this is the busiest time of the year in the tourism industry,
18.
we would like to invite you to our office at Winston Airport instead. It is a little far from your current workplace, but we will cover all of your travel expenses. Don't be ------- to tell us if this is inconvenient.
19.

------- time efficiency, please send us two letters of reference beforehand, so that
20.
we can prepare for the interview. The more information about your career we have, the less time we will need for the interview. Would you mind calling us at your earliest convenience to let us know your schedule?

We look forward to meeting you soon.

Sincerely,
William Taylor, Branch Manager, Nat East Travel

Q17. (A) schedule
(B) be scheduled
(C) be scheduling
(D) have been scheduled

Q18. (A) We have an increasing number of tourists.
(B) There were many applications for the position.
(C) The interview was to be held at the head office.
(D) The branch is always short-staffed.

Q19. (A) delighted　　(B) surprised　　(C) afraid　　(D) eligible

Q20. (A) In　　(B) On　　(C) For　　(D) At

設問パターン②

　Unit 3 で説明された「1. 全体の内容を問うパターン」の問題の一部は「解答するのに最も時間がかかる問題」と考えられます。なぜでしょう。

　まずそれらの設問の形ですが、**What is suggested / implied / indicated / mentioned / stated / true about ～?** となっています。では、「～について、何がわかるのか?」「～について、何が示されているか?」という問題の答えを選ぶ際、私たちは何をしなければならないでしょうか…そう、**4つの選択肢1つ1つを文書と照らし合わせる必要がある**のです。しかも、文中の表現がそのまま選択肢になっていることは極めてまれで、ほとんどが別の表現に言い換えられています。また、照らし合わせる文書の範囲が広いほど時間もかかります。

　本番では、**このような問題に時間を使いすぎないよう**、くれぐれも注意してください。

▶ Part 7 Single Passage

次の英文を読んで、設問に対する答えとして最も適切なものを選択肢の中から選びましょう。

Employment Contract

Star Ways Co., Ltd. (the "Company") and Shelly Wood (the "Employee") hereby enter into the following contract of employment.

1. **Employment Period**

   The period of employment shall be from 1 April, 2021 to 31 March, 2022 (one year with the possibility of renewal).

2. **Renewal of Contract**

   The contract may be renewed. It shall be determined by the following factors.

   (1) Volume of work to be done at the time the term of contract expires

   (2) Employee's work record and work attitude

   (3) Business performance of the Company

3. **Place of Employment: 52 Anson Road, Victoria Park, Bristol BS1 1DB**

4. **Responsibilities and Job Description**

   Prepare company newsletter for overseas operations, check English contracts, interpret for senior executives, assist with departmental work, such as planning strategies for the overseas subsidiaries and affiliated companies.

---

5. Work Hours

9:00 a.m. to 5:00 p.m. (Rest time: 12:00 p.m. to 1:00 p.m.)

6. Holidays

Holidays include Saturdays, Sundays, national holidays, from the afternoon of 30 December to 4 January, and summer holidays (five days during the months of July and August).

7. Overtime Work

Applicable

8. Paid Holidays

The Employee may take twelve paid holidays at any time except for weekdays during the period between 15 March and 31 March. Unused paid holidays may be carried over to the following year only.

9. Prohibition of Dual Employment

The Employee may not be employed by another company for any reasons.

...

Q21. In which department does Shelly Wood most likely work?

(A) Accounting   (B) Sales

(C) International   (D) Personnel

Q22. What is the Employee NOT responsible for at the Company?

(A) Editing house journals (B) Making contracts

(C) Assisting executives   (D) Reviewing documents

Q23. The word "affiliated" in paragraph 5, line 4, is closest in meaning to

(A) associated   (B) domestic

(C) incorporated   (D) parent

Q24. When is the Employee unable to take a holiday?

(A) On Tuesday, 7 July   (B) On Wednesday, 11 September

(C) On Saturday, 21 March   (D) On Friday, 27 March

Q25. What is suggested about Shelly Wood?

(A) She wants to extend her contract.

(B) She speaks multiple languages.

(C) She does not have to work overtime.

(D) She has a degree from graduate school.

▶ ボキャブラリーアルファ 4 Employment

この章のトピックでよく出る単語と表現です。日本語訳を見ながら英単語を声に出して言ってみましょう。

●雇用のトピックに出てくる単語 1-64

1 □ **salary** [sǽl(ə)ri]	名	給料
2 □ **attainment** [ətéinmənt]	名	到達、成就
3 □ **deadline** [dédlàin]	名	締め切り
4 □ **burden** [bə́:(r)dn]	名	重荷、重責
5 □ **judge** [dʒʌ́dʒ]	動	裁く、審判を下す
6 □ **respondent** [rispándənt]	名	回答者
7 □ **relinquish** [rilíŋkwiʃ]	動	放棄する、手放す
8 □ **promotion** [prəmóuʃən]	名	昇進、販売促進
9 □ **volunteer** [vὰləntíə(r)]	名	志願者、ボランティア
10 □ **incorporate** [inkɔ́:(r)pərèit]	動	組み込む
11 □ **rely** [rilái]	動	頼る
12 □ **competitor** [kəmpétətə(r)]	名	競合他社
13 □ **individual** [ìndəvídʒuəl]	形	個人の
14 □ **apprentice** [əpréntis]	名	見習い
15 □ **overview** [óuvə(r)vjù:]	名	概要、概略
16 □ **arrive** [əráiv]	動	到着する
17 □ **form** [fɔ́:(r)m]	名	記入式の書式、フォーム
18 □ **description** [diskrípʃən]	名	描写、解説
19 □ **responsibility** [rispὰnsəbíləti]	名	責任
20 □ **advanced** [ədvǽnst]	形	高度な

●雇用のトピックに出てくる表現 1-65

21 □ **temporary worker**	臨時雇い
22 □ **glass ceiling**	ガラスの天井
23 □ **paid vacation**	有給休暇
24 □ **minimum wage**	最低賃金
25 □ **labor union**	労働組合
26 □ **career track**	昇進コース
27 □ **nursery school**	保育園
28 □ **lifetime employment**	終身雇用
29 □ **terms and conditions**	条件
30 □ **work shift**	交替制勤務

UNIT **5** **Entertainment**

▶**Key Vocabulary**
 1-66

この章に出てくる下の英単語の中から日本語訳に当てはまる記号を（　）に記入しましょう。
答え合わせをしたら音声を聞いて英単語を声に出して読み、つづりを書き込み覚えましょう。

●エンターテイメントのトピックに出てくる単語

1.	指揮者	（　　）		9.	熟練の	（　　）	
2.	通路	（　　）		10.	〜に関して	（　　）	
3.	講堂	（　　）		11.	購入する	（　　）	
4.	提出する	（　　）		12.	応募者	（　　）	
5.	運営陣	（　　）		13.	無料の	（　　）	
6.	有名な	（　　）		14.	開催地	（　　）	
7.	業績	（　　）		15.	通知する	（　　）	
8.	貢献する	（　　）		16.	売り込む	（　　）	

a. administration **b.** complimentary **c.** contribute **d.** promote

e. conductor **f.** notify **g.** renowned **h.** aisle

i. venue **j.** accomplished **k.** applicant **l.** auditorium

m. purchase **n.** submit **o.** regarding **p.** achievement

LISTENING SECTION

Strategy for Part 1 《写真描写問題の解き方》

風景、室内の写真② 物の状況を判断しよう

下の Warming-Up の写真を見ながら物の状況を考えましょう。

●風景、室内の写真では、物の状態、状況を説明する表現が頻出します。写真の中に見
えるものが音声で聞こえてきても、すぐに正解にせず、その状況が正しいかを判断し
ましょう。

  1-67

音声を聞いて（　　　）内の語を穴埋めし、
正しい答えはどれか選びましょう。

(A) There is a (　　　　　) behind the bed.
(B) (　　　　　) have been put by the door.
(C) The (　　　　　) is now being played.
(D) A (　　　) has been placed near the
piano.　　　　　正しい答え　(A) (B) (C) (D)

41

▶ Part 1 Photographs

英文を聞き、4つの中から最も適切な描写を選びましょう。

Q1.   **Q2.**

Ⓐ Ⓑ Ⓒ Ⓓ

Ⓐ Ⓑ Ⓒ Ⓓ

Strategy for Part 2 ≪応答問題の解き方≫

一般疑問文① Do you ～ ?

　一般疑問文に対する答え方は例えば、中学校の英語の授業では Do you have a pen? に対して Yes, I do. や No, I don't. が基本的な答え方だと習いました。しかし TOEIC L&R においては、そのような基本的な答え方はひっかけ問題の誤答選択肢として頻出します。注意しましょう。

🔵 Warming-Up   1-70

音声を聞いて、疑問文とその答えの意味を記入しましょう。

Q: Do you have time to eat something now?

　(　　　　　　　　　　　　　　　　　　　　　　　　　　　　　　　　　　)

A: I'm sorry. I need to finish the proposal before the meeting.

　(　　　　　　　　　　　　　　　　　　　　　　　　　　　　　　　　　　)

▶ Part 2 Question-Response

設問に対する応答として、最も適切なものを選びましょう。

Q3. Mark your answer on your answer sheet.　　Ⓐ Ⓑ Ⓒ

Q4. Mark your answer on your answer sheet.　　Ⓐ Ⓑ Ⓒ

Q5. Mark your answer on your answer sheet.　　Ⓐ Ⓑ Ⓒ

Q6. Mark your answer on your answer sheet.　　Ⓐ Ⓑ Ⓒ

Strategy for Part 3 ≪会話問題の解き方≫

3ターンの会話問題① 会話が長くなっても集中力を保ち続けよう

Part 3 の会話は男→女→男→女、もしくは女→男→女→男の2ターンであることが多いですが、さらに長くなる場合でも「あいさつ」→「問題」→「問題解決」や、「あいさつ」→「出来事」→「次の行動」などの流れがあります。あらかじめ設問から必要な情報を予測し、集中力を保ち続けましょう。

Warming-Up

例えば次のような設問があったら音声はどのような会話だと予測できるか、（ ）内に記入しましょう。

What does the man ask the woman to do?

→男性が女性に何かを（　　　　　　　　　　　　　　　）頼んでいることがわかる。

▶ Part 3 Short Conversation

 1-75,76

会話文を聞いて、各設問に対する最も適切な答えを4つの選択肢から選びましょう。

Q7. What did the customer hand in?

    (A) A questionnaire   (B) A seating list

    (C) A script   (D) A leaflet

Q8. Where are the customers waiting for the show?

    (A) The administration office   (B) Inside the building

    (C) Outside the building   (D) The waiting room

Q9. Who is the man talking to?

    (A) Photographers   (B) Management

    (C) Stage carpenters   (D) The performers

Strategy for Part 4 《説明文問題の解き方》

トークの「展開」はほぼ決まっている！④

「Part 4 で聴くのは全て『トーク』のはずなのに、その中で、さらに "talk" って何？」
…こんな風に思っている人はいませんか。確かに Part 4 に登場するトークの一種に、「トーク (talk)」があります。トークが始まる直前の男性ナレーションで "the following talk" と聞こえたら…まずは「**その場を仕切る人のセリフ**」と考えてみてください。

🔵 Warming-Up 🎵 1-77

次の、説明文（トーク）に入る前の音声を、スクリプトを見ながら聞き、正しいものをすべて選び、○で囲みましょう。

「音声スクリプト」 "Questions 10 through 12 refer to the following talk."

この音声が聞こえた場合、トーク場面の例として、（ガイドツアー・オリエンテーション・授賞式・歓迎会・送別会）などが挙げられます。

▶ Part 4 Short Talk

 1-78,79

説明文を聞いて、各設問に対する最も適切な答えを4つの選択肢から選びましょう。

Q10. Where does the speaker most likely work?

    (A) At an art museum

    (B) At city hall

    (C) At an international organization

    (D) At a construction company

Q11. What does the woman imply when she says, "I don't need to tell you about his achievements here, right"?

    (A) People are not interested in him.

    (B) People already know a lot about him.

    (C) He will introduce himself.

    (D) He does not want to wait.

Q12. According to the speaker, what happened in 1990?

    (A) The project was planned.

    (B) The museum was completed.

    (C) The company was established.

    (D) The competition was held.

44

READING SECTION

Strategy for Part 5 ≪短文穴埋め問題のための Grammar ≫

動詞の形問題⑤ 「現在分詞」も「過去分詞」も形容詞の働きをする

　短文穴埋め問題の選択肢として頻出する **-ing 形**と **-ed 形**はどちらも動詞が変化した形です。それぞれ「**現在分詞**」「**過去分詞**」と呼ばれて、文の中では形容詞として働きます。

☆「**現在分詞**」（〜する、〜している）

　① 前から修飾：**現在分詞が単独で名詞を修飾**する場合

　　That was an **interesting** movie.
　　　　　　　　　現在分詞　　名詞

　　（それは面白い映画でした。）

　② 後ろから修飾：≪**現在分詞 + 語句**≫が名詞を修飾する場合

　　A bus **carrying** passengers stopped at the terminal.
　　　名詞　　現在分詞 + 語句

　　（乗客を乗せたバスはターミナルで止まりました。）

☆「**過去分詞**」（〜される、〜されている）

　① 前から修飾：**過去分詞が単独で名詞を修飾**する場合

　　The police found the **stolen** passport in the office.
　　　　　　　　　　　　過去分詞　　名詞

　　（警察はそのオフィスで盗まれたパスポートを見つけました。）

　② 後ろから修飾：≪**過去分詞 + 語句**≫が名詞を修飾する場合

　　I have a room **reserved** for two.
　　　　　　　名詞　　過去分詞 + 語句

　　（2 人のために予約した部屋があります。）

🖰 Warming-Up

以下は感情の動きを表す動詞です。「その気持ちにさせる」の場合は現在分詞、「その気持ちにさせられる」場合は過去分詞を使います。（　　）に意味を書きましょう。

(1) boring　　　（　　　　　　　）　bored　　　　（　　　　　　　）
(2) amazing　　（　　　　　　　）　amazed　　　（　　　　　　　）
(3) embarrassing（　　　　　　　）　embarrassed（　　　　　　　）
(4) tiring　　　（　　　　　　　）　tired　　　　（　　　　　　　）
(5) exciting　　（　　　　　　　）　excited　　　（　　　　　　　）

▶ Part 5 Incomplete Sentences

空所に入る最も適切な語句を選びましょう。

Q13. The audition seems very (   ).

    (A) challenge   (B) being challenged   (C) challenged   (D) challenging

Q14. The city hall is planning to invite an (   ) musician.

    (A) accomplished   (B) accomplish   (C) accomplishing   (D) accomplishes

Q15. The student raised questions (   ) the importance of habits.

    (A) regards   (B) best regards   (C) regarding   (D) regarded

Q16. (   ) Robert's work experience as a doctor, it was no surprise that the manager put him in charge of the health program.

    (A) Given   (B) Giving   (C) Having given   (D) Being giving

Strategy for Part 6 ≪長文穴埋め問題の解き方≫

　　Part 6 と Part 7 の文書の違いの一つに、その「スタイル（様式)」があります。例えばスマートフォンの画面の絵など、Part 7 の文書が比較的色々なスタイルをとるのに対して、Part 6 の文書のスタイルは地味で、文書のタイトルすら書いていないことも少なくありません。Part 6 の文書の種類の一つは「**広告（advertisement)**」ですが、100語前後のシンプルな文書ですので、それほどたくさんの情報は入っておらず、最後まで読み切ってもさほど時間はかからないはずです。まずは Part 6 の**解答目安時間を「一文書（4問）につき2分30秒」**としてみてはいかがでしょうか。

▶ Part 6 Text Completion

次の英文を読んで、選択肢の中から空所に入る最も適切な語句を選びましょう。

The Winter Musical Festival is Coming Soon!

First Planning Co., Ltd. is pleased to inform you that our annual musical evening is coming back to Stanstead Town. This winter, Stanstead Operetta, which is now an internationally famous theater company, will stage some fantastic musicals in ------- hometown. Tickets will be available from the town's Web site
17.
from next week.

Also, there is a special event this time. For ------- of you interested in ------- actors
18.   **19.**
and actresses are doing backstage, only 20 people are allowed to enter for free.
-------. If you are interested, please let us know in the comment box when you
20.
purchase your ticket online.

Q17. (A) it   (B) its   (C) them   (D) they

Q18. (A) this   (B) these   (C) that   (D) those

Q19. (A) which   (B) who   (C) what   (D) whose

Q20. (A) It is a rare opportunity.
    (B) It will cost an additional fee.
    (C) The price depends on the number of applicants.
    (D) Titles of the musicals will be announced soon.

設問パターン③

　Unit 2 で紹介した Part 7 の設問の種類のうちの、「2. 個別の詳細を問うパターン」は、「文書の中の具体的な情報を見つけて理解する問題」とも言えます。

　こちらは基本的に**解答に時間がかかりません**。例えば「Michael Burns は誰ですか？」という問題があるとします。この問題のヒントを見つけるために、おそらく多くの人は Michael Burns という名前を探すと思います。そこにヒントさえ見つかれば、正解を選ぶことはそれほど難しくありません。現在 Part 7 を苦手にしている人は、まずこのタイプの問題に正解できるよう練習してはいかがでしょう。

　では、どうすればヒントを見つけやすくできるでしょうか。そう、やはり「**設問を解き始める前に、一通り文書に目を通す**」ことがお勧めです。

 ## Part 7 Double Passages

次の英文を読んで、設問に対する答えとして最も適切なものを選択肢の中から選びましょう。

---

http://www.xxxx/xxxx/

A great chance to get a ticket!

Star Gate Music Co., Ltd. is delighted to announce that we will provide local residents of the town with 100 complimentary tickets for our annual summer rock music festival.

Since the first festival was held, Dales Town has been kindly advertising our events in advance, allowing us to use its spacious courtyard as well as operating free shuttles between the venue and the station on the day of the event.

With all our gratitude to the town, we have arranged the seats and some refreshments for you. There will be a ballot if we receive over 100 applications. You can make an entry on our Web site, www.sgmusic.com, no later than July 3. Please note that applicants must be living in the town. The winners will be notified by e-mail by July 21.

E-mail

To: John Hammond <jhammond@arther.net>
From: Perry Adams <padams@sgmusic.com>
Date: July 19
Subject: Result of the ballot
Attachment: The Summer Rock Festival

Dear Mr. Hammond,

Congratulations! We are pleased to inform you that you have won a ticket for the summer rock music festival. Please find the attached ticket, print it out and bring it to the ticket office on the day of the event. Some refreshments will be available for you at the security lodge at the entrance. Furthermore, you can ride on the shuttle service by presenting the ticket to the driver.

Finally, we would appreciate it if you could e-mail us a review of the festival, so that we can post it on our Web site.

Thank you in advance.

Perry Adams
Sales Representative

Q21. What is the purpose of the Web page?

(A) To invite residents to the event

(B) To promote a music band

(C) To notify a schedule change

(D) To announce the opening day

Q22. On the Web page, the word "complimentary" in paragraph 1, line 2, is closest in meaning to

(A) valuable   (B) rare   (C) discounted   (D) free

Q23. What did Dales Town NOT do?

(A) Provide light meals

(B) Offer transportation services

(C) Open its facilities

(D) Advertise the festival

Q24. What is John Hammond asked to do?

(A) Contact the town hall

(B) Purchase a ticket online

(C) Print the attached document

(D) Use public transportation

Q25. What did John Hammond most likely do before July 3?

(A) Visited the venue

(B) Advertised the event

(C) Applied for a draw

(D) Moved into the town

▶ ボキャブラリーアルファ 5 Entertainment

この章のトピックでよく出る単語と表現です。日本語訳を見ながら英単語を声に出して言ってみましょう。

●エンターテインメントのトピックに出てくる単語 1-80

	単語	発音	品詞	意味
1 □	curio	[kjú(ə)ріòu]	名	骨董品
2 □	instinct	[ínstiŋ(k)t]	名	本能
3 □	action	[ǽkʃən]	名	行動
4 □	rehearse	[rihə́:(r)s]	動	下げいこする、リハーサルをする
5 □	perform	[pə(r)fɔ́:(r)m]	動	演じる
6 □	appreciate	[əprí:ʃièit]	動	感謝する
7 □	random	[rǽndəm]	形	でたらめな
8 □	valid	[vǽlid]	形	有効な
9 □	subscribe	[səbskráib]	動	申し込む、購読する
10 □	majority	[məʤɔ́(:)rəti]	名	大多数
11 □	unveil	[ʌnvéil]	動	発表する
12 □	thoroughly	[θə́:rouli]	副	徹底的に
13 □	subjective	[səbʤéktiv]	形	主観的な
14 □	feedback	[fí:dbæ̀k]	名	意見、フィードバック
15 □	audience	[ɔ́:diəns]	名	視聴者
16 □	review	[rivjú:]	名	見直し、批評
17 □	taste	[téist]	名	味、好み
18 □	favor	[féivə(r)]	動	より好む

●エンターテインメントのトピックに出てくる表現 1-81

	表現	意味
19 □	sign up for	～に登録する
20 □	historical figure	歴史上の人物
21 □	dress code	服装規定
22 □	live coverage	実況中継
23 □	book coupon	図書券
24 □	buffet party	立食パーティー
25 □	Ferris wheel	観覧車
26 □	feature story	特集記事
27 □	check box	回答用ボックス、チェックボックス
28 □	local specialty	地方の名産
29 □	botanical garden	植物園
30 □	Medieval Ages	中世

UNIT **6** Shopping / Purchases

▶ Key Vocabulary 1-82

この章に出てくる下の英単語の中から日本語訳に当てはまる記号を（　）に記入しましょう。
答え合わせをしたら音声を聞いて英単語を声に出して読み、つづりを書き込み覚えましょう。

●買い物 / 購入のトピックに出てくる単語

1.	追加の	（　）	9.	好み	（　）
2.	お知らせ	（　）	10.	電化製品	（　）
3.	保証する	（　）	11.	除外する	（　）
4.	一時的に	（　）	12.	発送する	（　）
5.	罰する	（　）	13.	調査する	（　）
6.	実施する	（　）	14.	その結果	（　）
7.	前任者	（　）	15.	欠陥のある	（　）
8.	まったく別な	（　）	16.	クーポン券	（　）

a. implement	**b.** distinct	**c.** exclude	**d.** additional
e. voucher	**f.** notification	**g.** defective	**h.** predecessor
i. guarantee	**j.** consequently	**k.** temporarily	**l.** examine
m. dispatch	**n.** preference	**o.** penalize	**p.** appliance

LISTENING SECTION

Strategy for Part 1 ≪写真描写問題の解き方≫

周辺の物が正解の場合

下の Warming-Up の写真を見ながら主語が何を表しているものが正解か、判断しましょう。

● 人物が一人だけ、もしくは複数の人物が写っていても、一人の人物が目立っていない場合、周辺のものを表した表現が正解になることがあります。選択肢の中でも単純に「人＋行動」を示すものが正解とは限らないことに注意しましょう。

 Warming-Up 1-83

音声を聞いて（　　）内の語を穴埋めし、
正しい答えはどれか選びましょう。

(A) The (　　　　) are examining a document.
(B) The (　　　) are being trimmed in the shop.
(C) The building is made of (　　　　).
(D) A lot of (　　　) are displayed on the shelves.

正しい答え　(A) (B) (C) (D)

51

▶ Part 1 Photographs

英文を聞き、4つの中から最も適切な描写を選びましょう。

Q1.

Ⓐ Ⓑ Ⓒ Ⓓ

Q2.

Ⓐ Ⓑ Ⓒ Ⓓ

Strategy for Part 2 《応答問題の解き方》

一般疑問文②　Are we〜？　Is he〜？

be 動詞で始まる一般疑問文でも典型的な答え方、例えば Yes, I am. No, he isn't. は誤答選択肢として出題されます。

 🎧 Warming-Up 1-86

音声を聞いて、疑問文とその答えの意味を記入しましょう。

Q: Are you supposed to open the front door today?

(   )

A: I should check whose shift it is.

(   )

▶ Part 2 Question-Response

 1-87,88,89,90

設問に対する応答として、最も適切なものを選びましょう。

Q3. Mark your answer on your answer sheet.　　Ⓐ Ⓑ Ⓒ

Q4. Mark your answer on your answer sheet.　　Ⓐ Ⓑ Ⓒ

Q5. Mark your answer on your answer sheet.　　Ⓐ Ⓑ Ⓒ

Q6. Mark your answer on your answer sheet.　　Ⓐ Ⓑ Ⓒ

Strategy for Part 3 《会話問題の解き方》

2人の会話問題③　What を含む設問

What で始まる疑問文には様々な種類があり、色々な内容について聞くことができます。従って、Part 3, Part 4 の設問の多くを占めると言えるでしょう。What is the conversation mainly about? 「この会話は主に何に関するものですか」など、会話全体に関する質問や、What will the speakers probably do next? 「話し手たちは次に何をすると考えられますか」のような、これから起こる事柄についての質問が出題されることもあります。

Warming-Up

次の設問を読んで、日本語に訳してから、会話の内容を予測しましょう。

　What does the man ask his boss to do?

　(　　　　　　　　　　　　　　　　　　　　　　　　　　　　　　　　　)

→ (　　　　　　　　) が (　　　　　　　　　　　) に何かを頼んでいるとわかる。

▶ Part 3 Short Conversation

 1-91,92

会話文を聞いて、各設問に対する最も適切な答えを4つの選択肢から選びましょう。

Q7. What did the woman get yesterday?

(A) A birthday card   (B) A name tag

(C) An e-mail notification   (D) A brochure

Q8. Approximately how much of a discount will the woman get for her purchases?

(A) Less than 10 percent   (B) 20 percent

(C) 40 percent   (D) More than 40 percent

Q9. What does the man suggest the woman do?

(A) Buy the bag soon   (B) Choose the color carefully

(C) Submit an application   (D) Calculate the percentage

Strategy for Part 4 ≪説明文問題の解き方≫

トークの「展開」はほぼ決まっている！⑤

　Part 4 でよく登場するトークの種類に「宣伝広告（advertisement）」があります。宣伝されるのは主に、①商品、②事業所（店、レストラン等）などです。続く設問では、**「何の広告なのか」**という**概要**を問われたり、「**割引**」「**特典**」「**期間**」などの**詳細情報**を問われたりすることが多々あります。

 Warming-Up 🎵1-93

次の、説明文に入る前の音声を、スクリプトを見ながら聞きましょう。

「音声スクリプト」"Questions 10 through 12 refer to the following advertisement."
この音声が聞こえ、設問に　"What type of business ～ ?" とある場合、何が問われているでしょうか。正しいものを１つ選び、○で囲みましょう。

（答え：会社名・会社の業種・会社の部署名・会社での役職）

▶ Part 4 Short Talk

 1-94,95

説明文を聞いて、各設問に対する最も適切な答えを４つの選択肢から選びましょう。

Q10. What type of business is probably being advertised?

 (A) A farmer's market   (B) A food company

 (C) A restaurant   (D) A grocery store

Q11. How can the listeners get a bigger discount?

 (A) By showing a coupon   (B) By purchasing local products

 (C) By presenting a card   (D) By donating to a charity

Q12. Look at the graphic. When will the renovation begin?

 (A) On June 2   (B) On July 4

 (C) On August 10   (D) On September 1

~ Schedule for the Summer Special Events ~

Event	Last Day
"For Your Homemade Dishes"	June 2
"Organic Tastes from the North"	July 4
"Tropical Fruits Fair"	August 10
"Coming of Autumn Week"	September 1

READING SECTION

Strategy for Part 5　≪短文穴埋め問題のための Grammar ≫

品詞識別問題①　「文の要素」を思い出そう

　選択肢が全て似ていて、同じ語幹の派生語が並んでいる場合、「品詞識別問題」です。選択肢の品詞の種類をチェックして、空所の役割を考えましょう。

The company wanted to improve product (　　　　) to meet consumers'
expectation.

　　(A) rely　　　　　　　〈動詞〉
　　(B) reliable　　　　　　〈形容詞〉
　　(C) reliably　　　　　　〈副詞〉
　　(D) reliability　　　　　〈名詞〉

空所の役割を考えるために「文の要素」を整理してみましょう。

S 〈主語〉Subject	動作主を表します。人や物事で、「…は、…が」と訳します。	
V 〈動詞〉Verb	動作や状態（…する、…である）を表します。	
O 〈目的語〉Object	動詞が働きかける対象。（…を、…に）を表す部分です。	
C 〈補語〉Complement	主語（S）や目的語（O）を説明する部分です。	

基本事項

☆目的語になるのは名詞、代名詞、名詞相当語句。補語になるのは名詞、形容詞などです。

☆「**名詞**」を修飾する場合→「**形容詞**」または「**名詞**」が入ります。

☆「**動詞**」「**形容詞**」「**副詞**」を修飾する場合→「**副詞**」が入ります。

この例題では product という名詞が空所を修飾する形となり、空所には名詞である reliability が入ります。正解は (D) です。

参考訳）その企業は顧客の期待に沿うために製品の信頼性を改善したいと考えている。

🔵 Warming-Up

　単語には名詞にも動詞にもなるものが多く存在します。以下はその一部です。左に名詞の意味、右に動詞の意味を記入しましょう。

(1) an increase	(	)	increase	(	)
(2) a survey	(	)	survey	(	)
(3) a question	(	)	question	(	)
(4) an implement	(	)	implement	(	)
(5) a contract	(	)	contract	(	)
(6) a plan	(	)	plan	(	)

Part 5 Incomplete Sentences

空所に入る最も適切な語句を選びましょう。

Q13. The shop owner (　　) a new policy yesterday that will penalize part-timers who are late for work without notice.

(A) implements　　(B) implemented　　(C) implementing　　(D) implementation

Q14. After launching its new model, the car manufacturer received (　　) that the navigation systems were not working properly.

(A) complaints　　(B) complainer　　(C) complained　　(D) complains

Q15. Simon's sales techniques are quite (　　) from his predecessor's.

(A) distinct　　(B) distinction　　(C) distinctively　　(D) distinguish

Q16. Increased sales of organic vegetables are (　　) of the current consumer preference for natural produce.

(A) indicate　　(B) indicating　　(C) indicated　　(D) indicative

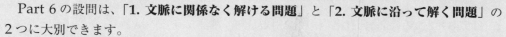

Strategy for Part 6 ≪長文穴埋め問題の解き方≫

　Part 6 の設問は、「**1. 文脈に関係なく解ける問題**」と「**2. 文脈に沿って解く問題**」の2つに大別できます。

　「**1. 文脈に関係なく解ける問題**」とは、言い換えると、**空欄の入っている文だけを読めば解ける問題**です。具体的には、「品詞を選ぶ問題」「前置詞を選ぶ問題」「関係代名詞を選ぶ問題」などが挙げられます。このような問題は、一つの文だけで解ける問題、つまり Part 5 の問題と同じです。一文書4問中たいてい1問は入っています。ほとんど時間はかかりませんので、テストで残り時間が少ない時でも、必ず解くことをお勧めします。

▶ Part 6 Text Completion

次の英文を読んで、選択肢の中から空所に入る最も適切な語句を選びましょう。

To: Customer Service <customer@bicstore.com>
From: Vincent Grace <vgrace@arriva.net>
Date: April 30
Subject: Missing items

I purchased a vacuum cleaner, AC15, from your online store last week. ------- **17.** ,
the paper filters for it were not enclosed in the box. ------- **18.** . However, it was
advertised that, during the sale, the complimentary filters would be offered with
the cleaner. Since I need to clean up my house for a party next week, I would
be grateful if you could ------- **19.** the packs immediately.

------- **20.** the above, I am quite satisfied with the item. I appreciate the affordable
prices you always offer and look forward to buying other home appliances from
this shop in the future.

Thank you.
Vincent

Q17. (A) Moreover   (B) Unfortunately   (C) Specifically   (D) Besides

Q18. (A) I was supposed to receive a call from you.
     (B) I thought I was eligible to get a full refund.
     (C) I understand that the pack is usually excluded.
     (D) I was so disappointed that I will never buy from you again.

Q19. (A) acquire   (B) present   (C) dispatch   (D) proceed

Q20. (A) Except for   (B) Because of   (C) According to   (D) Along with

ダブル・パッセージ型

　Part 7 では、設問 176 から設問 185 まで、2 つの文書を読んで解答する設問が 5 問 × 2 セット続きます。このような「ダブル・パッセージ型」は、読むべき文書量が多く、また Reading Section の終盤に出てくるので、漠然と「難しい」というイメージを持つ人が多いようです。

　しかし実際に 2 つの文書からヒントを見つけないと解けない設問は、**1 セット（5 問）中、1, 2 問しかありません**。つまり、その他の設問は、どちらかの文書でヒントを見つければ解けるということです。設問にある「According to the e-mail,」など、**どちらの文書にヒントがあるのかを示す語句に注意**し、効率よくヒントを見つける練習をするとよいでしょう。

▶ Part 7 Double Passages

次の英文を読んで、設問に対する答えとして最も適切なものを選択肢の中から選びましょう。

To: Customer Care Team <customercare@worldpc.co.uk>
From: Megan Paul <meganpaul@arriva.net>
Date: 15 May
Subject: Refund process

I purchased a touch-screen tablet at my local World PC shop on the 3rd of May. Unfortunately, the screen had a tiny scratch on it, I filled out the return form attached to the item, and sent both the product and the form to the address shown in the instructions on the same day.

Although I followed your return policy correctly and completed the return process within the required time limit, as of today, I have not received a refund from you. Could you please check the status of my refund and update me as soon as possible?

Thank you in advance.
Megan

To: Megan Paul <meganpaul@arriva.net>
From: Sean Little <seanlittle@worldpc.co.uk>
Date: 16 May
Subject: Re: Refund process

Dear Ms. Paul,

Thank you very much for your continued patronage. I am writing in response to your e-mail that we received yesterday regarding the refund process. We immediately checked it out on our online data-base and examined the purchase records of the Vermont branch. Consequently, it turned out that the staff at our warehouse in Springfield failed to input some important information from your purchase.

We apologize for any inconvenience this mistake has caused you. Now that we have confirmed the item has been returned, we will send a full refund to your bank account within today. In addition, as a token of our apology, I am attaching a 50 percent discount coupon for a future purchase at any of our shops.

Kind regards,
Sean Little, Customer Care Team Representative, World PC Co., Ltd.

Q21. According to the first e-mail, what is the problem?
(A) A shipment has not arrived yet.
(B) A receipt of purchase is not enclosed.
(C) An item is defective.
(D) A shop has been relocated.

Q22. What did Megan Paul most likely do on 15 May?
(A) Completed a form
(B) Dispatched an item
(C) Placed another order
(D) Checked her bank account

Q23. According to the second e-mail, what will Megan Paul receive?
(A) A voucher
(B) A bank statement
(C) A replacement
(D) An invoice

Q24. The word "examined" in paragraph 1, line 3, in the second e-mail, is closest in meaning to
(A) preserved
(B) passed
(C) collected
(D) inspected

Q25. What is indicated about Megan Paul?
(A) She has not shopped at the World PC Co., Ltd. before.
(B) She lives near the Vermont branch.
(C) She has recently moved into Springfield.
(D) She made a mistake in inputting data.

ボキャブラリーアルファ 6 Shopping/Purchases

この章のトピックでよく出る単語と表現です。日本語訳を見ながら英単語を声に出して言ってみましょう。

●買い物 / 購入のトピックに出てくる単語　　CD 1-96

1 ☐ **profit** [práfət]	名	利益
2 ☐ **depreciation** [diprí:ʃièiʃən]	名	減価償却
3 ☐ **browse** [bráuz]	動	見て回る
4 ☐ **available** [əvéiləbl]	形	入手可能な
5 ☐ **combine** [kəmbáin]	動	組み合わせる
6 ☐ **familiar** [fəmíljə(r)]	形	なじみの、見慣れた
7 ☐ **category** [kǽtəgɔ̀:ri]	名	カテゴリー、部門
8 ☐ **equivalent** [ikwív(ə)lənt]	形	同等の
9 ☐ **shipping** [ʃípiŋ]	名	発送
10 ☐ **predict** [pridíkt]	動	予想する、予期する
11 ☐ **reimburse** [rì:imbə́:s]	動	返金する
12 ☐ **appeal** [əpí:l]	名	魅力
13 ☐ **merchandise** [mə́:(r)tʃəndàiz]	名	商品
14 ☐ **separately** [sép(ə)rətli]	副	分かれて、ばらばらに
15 ☐ **compromise** [kámprəmàiz]	動	妥協する
16 ☐ **track** [trǽk]	動	追跡する
17 ☐ **urge** [ə́:(r)dʒ]	動	駆り立てる、促す
18 ☐ **relaxation** [rì:lækséiʃən]	名	くつろぎ

●買い物 / 購入のトピックに出てくる表現　　CD 1-97

19 ☐ **sell out**	売り切れ
20 ☐ **supermarket chain**	スーパーのチェーン
21 ☐ **back order**	取り寄せ注文
22 ☐ **previous balance**	前回未納分
23 ☐ **petty cash**	小口現金
24 ☐ **competitive price**	割安価格
25 ☐ **order status**	注文状況
26 ☐ **product line**	製品ライン
27 ☐ **fitting room**	試着室
28 ☐ **fiscal year**	事業年度、会計年度
29 ☐ **online shopping**	ネットショッピング
30 ☐ **top-end**	最高級の

UNIT **7** Sports / Health

▶ **Key Vocabulary**

 2-01

この章に出てくる下の英単語の中から日本語訳に当てはまる記号を（ ）に記入しましょう。
答え合わせをしたら音声を聞いて英単語を声に出して読み、つづりを書き込み覚えましょう。

● スポーツ / 健康のトピックに出てくる単語

1.	障害物	（　　）		9.	延期する	（　　）	
2.	煮え立つ	（　　）		10.	～のため	（　　）	
3.	抜歯	（　　）		11.	開業医	（　　）	
4.	入れ歯	（　　）		12.	確実にする	（　　）	
5.	チェックする	（　　）		13.	伝染性の	（　　）	
6.	配布物	（　　）		14.	改装	（　　）	
7.	偶然	（　　）		15.	評価する	（　　）	
8.	効率的な	（　　）		16.	前もって	（　　）	

a. denture	**b.** efficient	**c.** ensure	**d.** boiling
e. postpone	**f.** practitioner	**g.** fortuity	**h.** extraction
i. beforehand	**j.** obstacle	**k.** infectious	**l.** evaluate
m. handout	**n.** refurbishment	**o.** tick	**p.** due to

LISTENING SECTION

Strategy for Part 1 ≪写真描写問題の解き方≫

似ている音の聞き取り①

下の Warming-Up の写真に出てくるものと似ている音を探しましょう。

● Part 1 では、写真の中に出てくるものと発音の似ている語が選択肢に出てくる問題
も頻出します。音を聞いただけできちんと判別できるように練習しておきましょう。

 2-02

音声を聞いて（　　）内の語を穴埋めし、
正しい答えはどれか選びましょう。

(A) People are (　　　　) riding in the woods.
(B) A man is watering the (　　　　) with a
hose.
(C) A man is being followed by a (　　　　).
(D) People are (　　　　　) their dogs.

正しい答え　(A) (B) (C) (D)

▶ Part 1 Photographs

英文を聞き、4つの中から最も適切な描写を選びましょう。

Q1.

Ⓐ Ⓑ Ⓒ Ⓓ

Q2.

Ⓐ Ⓑ Ⓒ Ⓓ

Strategy for Part 2 ≪応答問題の解き方≫

一般疑問文③　正解のパターンを知ろう

　質問に対して「わかりません」と答える場合や、質問に対して質問で返す場合でも、会話の流れがナチュラルであれば、Part 2 においては正解となります。

 Warming-Up 💿2-05

音声を聞いて、疑問文とその正解のパターンの答えの意味を記入しましょう。

Q: Do you know how to get to the hospital?

　(　　　　　　　　　　　　　　　　　　　　　　　　　　　　　　　)

A: I have no idea.　◎正解　(　　　　　　　　　　　　　　　　　　　)

A: Shall I ask someone else?　◎正解　(　　　　　　　　　　　　　　　)

A: Is there something wrong with you? ◎正解　(　　　　　　　　　　　　)

▶ Part 2 Question-Response

設問に対する応答として、最も適切なものを選びましょう。

Q3. Mark your answer on your answer sheet.　　Ⓐ Ⓑ Ⓒ

Q4. Mark your answer on your answer sheet.　　Ⓐ Ⓑ Ⓒ

Q5. Mark your answer on your answer sheet.　　Ⓐ Ⓑ Ⓒ

Q6. Mark your answer on your answer sheet.　　Ⓐ Ⓑ Ⓒ

Strategy for Part 3 《会話問題の解き方》

2人の会話問題④ Where を含む設問

　Part 3 の設問のうち、Where で始まるのは Where is this conversation taking place?「この会話はどこで行われていますか」Where do the speakers probably work?「話し手はおそらくどこで働いていますか」など、会話全体に関する質問が多いです。また単純に Where is the library located?「図書館はどこにありますか」など、会話に出てくる場所について聞かれることもあります。

🔵 Warming-Up

次の設問を読んで、日本語に訳してから、会話の内容を予測しましょう。

　Where does the woman probably work?
　(　　　　　　　　　　　　　　　　　　　　　　　　　　　　　　)
→女性が（＿＿＿＿＿＿＿＿＿＿＿＿）いるとわかる。

▶ Part 3 Short Conversation

 2-10,11

会話文を聞いて、各設問に対する最も適切な答えを4つの選択肢から選びましょう。

Q7. Where is the man probably calling from?
　(A) The train station 　　　(B) His own car
　(C) The dental office 　　　(D) His house

Q8. What will Dr. Stewart do this morning?
　(A) See the first client 　　　(B) Call traffic control
　(C) Make a client's denture 　　　(D) Look for a shortcut

Q9. What time does the conversation probably take place?
　(A) 6:00 a.m. 　　　(B) 9:30 a.m.
　(C) 10:30 a.m. 　　　(D) 11:00 a.m.

「図表問題」の解き方①

2016 年 5 月の公開テストから「新形式」に変わった TOEIC L&R、Part 3 と Part 4 では新たに「**図表問題（グラフや図などを見ながら解く問題）**」が登場しました。

設問が必ず "Look at the graphic." で始まるこの図表問題ですが、テストでは **Part 3 と Part 4 に、合計 5 問出題**されます（例：Part 3 に 3 問、Part 4 に 2 問）。「図表を見ながら聴いて選択肢も選ぶなんて、難しそう」という印象を持っている方はいませんか。

実はこの種類の問題には、解く前の心構えが必要です。①事前に選択肢と図表をチェック、②「**選択肢に並んでいる語句は、トークからは聞こえてこない**」と考えましょう。もしそれらがトークから聞こえてしまったらどうでしょう。図表は不要になりませんか。

🔴 Warming-Up

図表に、「商品番号」と「在庫数」が載っているとします。設問の選択肢に、「商品番号」が並んでいる場合、リスニング音声から実際に聞こえてくるのは、何でしょうか。正しいものを 1 つ選び、○で囲みましょう。（答え：商品番号・商品名・在庫数・価格）

▶ Part 4 Short Talk

 2-12,13

説明文を聞いて、各設問に対する最も適切な答えを 4 つの選択肢から選びましょう。

Q10. What type of product is being introduced?

    (A) A diet food   (B) A medicine

    (C) A smartphone   (D) An application

Q11. Who most likely is the speaker?

    (A) A medical doctor   (B) A company employee

    (C) An event organizer   (D) A fitness instructor

Q12. Look at the graphic. Where is "Your Health Level" on the screen?

    (A) Position A

    (B) Position B

    (C) Position C

    (D) Position D

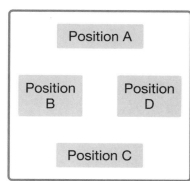

READING SECTION

Strategy for Part 5 《短文穴埋め問題のための Grammar》

品詞識別問題②　「基本5文型」と「第2文型」、「第3文型」の見分け方

★「基本5文型」はやっぱり大事。

文の要素を使って、基本5文型をまとめると次のようになります。

第1文型（S+V）　　　　例：She smiles.（彼女は微笑みます。）

第2文型（S+V+C）　　　例：I am young.（私は若いです。）

第3文型（S+V+O）　　　例：She loves her son.（彼女は息子を愛しています。）

第4文型（S+V+O+O）　 例：I gave you some advice.
　　　　　　　　　　　　　（あなたにアドバイスをしました。）

第5文型（S+V+O+C）　 例：She keeps it secret.
　　　　　　　　　　　　　（彼女はそのことを秘密にしています。）

「第2文型」と「第3文型」の見分け方

この5つの文型の中で、重要で、混同しやすいのが「第2文型」と「第3文型」です。

第2文型（S+V+C）　**SとCはイコールの関係です。**

Paul　 is　 tall.
〈S〉　〈V〉　〈C:形容詞〉　　**Paul = tall**

（ポールは背が高いです。）

第3文型（S+V+O）

　O は「…を」「…に」の部分です。**SとOはイコールの関係ではありません。**

Paul　 loves　 her.
〈S〉　〈V〉　〈O〉　　**Paul ≠ her**

（ポールは彼女を愛しています。）

🔵 Warming-Up

次の文は第1文型から第5文型のどれに当てはまるでしょうか。日本語訳を書いた後に
文型を（　）に記入しましょう。

(1) I found the novel easy. （　　　　　　　　　　　　　　）（第＿＿文型）

(2) Last week, retail sales rose significantly.

　　（　　　　　　　　　　　　　　　　　　　　　　　　　　）（第＿＿文型）

(3) They invited Dr. Smith to the party.

　　（　　　　　　　　　　　　　　　　　　　　　　　　　　）（第＿＿文型）

(4) She became a dentist. （　　　　　　　　　　　　　）（第＿＿文型）

(5) I gave my father flowers on his birthday.

　　（　　　　　　　　　　　　　　　　　　　　　　　　　　）（第＿＿文型）

▶ Part 5 Incomplete Sentences

空所に入る最も適切な語句を選びましょう。

Q13. Ms. Wilford considers it (   ) to have booked the premium seat at such short notice.

(A) fortuity   (B) fortune   (C) fortunate   (D) fortunately

Q14. It is important to make (   ) use of cleaning robots.

(A) efficient   (B) efficiency   (C) efficiently   (D) efficiencies

Q15. The camp will be postponed until the weekend due to poor weather (   ).

(A) permission   (B) climate   (C) conditions   (D) cloudy

Q16. All medical practitioners are advised to wear the masks, which ensures (   ) protection from infectious disease.

(A) complete   (B) completely   (C) completed   (D) completing

Strategy for Part 6 ≪長文穴埋め問題の解き方≫

　　空欄穴埋め問題という点では同様の Part 5 と Part 6 ですが、Unit 6 でご紹介した、Part 6 の 2 種類の設問タイプのうちの「2. 文脈に沿って解く問題」の存在が両者の大きな違いの一つです。

　　このタイプは、「空欄の入っている文だけでは解けず、前後の文を読む必要が生じる問題」です。具体的には、「文と文をつなぐ語句（接続副詞）を選ぶ問題」「代名詞を選ぶ問題」「語彙を選ぶ問題」「動詞の形（時制・態）を選ぶ問題」などが挙げられます。

　　最近の TOEIC L&R の **Part 6 では、大半がこのタイプの問題**になっています。まずは文書を一気に読み通してから設問にとりかかった方が効率よく解答できる、と言える所以です。

▶ Part 6 Text Completion

次の英文を読んで、選択肢の中から空所に入る最も適切な語句を選びましょう。

Renewal Opening of Stirling Aquatic Center

STIRLING (17 June) – Stirling City announced yesterday that the Municipal Aquatic Center has been reopened after a six-month refurbishment. The new building has three floors. On the first floor, two new swimming pools ------- **17.** . One is a shallow pool for young children, and ------- **18.** is for walking in the water only. On the second floor, spectator stands with 500 seats have been newly constructed. Renewable energy sources have also been installed. There are now 100 solar panels on the rooftop generating clean energy for the facilities. The gym in the basement has nearly doubled in size with a ------- **19.** of training machines. Waiting times to use the equipment are expected to be reduced. ------- **20.** .

Q17. (A) added
(B) have been added
(C) is added
(D) will be added

Q18. (A) the other
(B) another
(C) others
(D) the others

Q19. (A) variety
(B) various
(C) vary
(D) variously

Q20. (A) The city hall will be closed for a month.
(B) The construction will be completed in a week.
(C) The convention center will be under renovation.
(D) The café by the reception will be available soon.

トリプル・パッセージ型

　Part 7 の最後、設問 186 から設問 200 までは、3 つの文書を読んで解答する設問が 5 問×3 セット出題されます。この「トリプル・パッセージ型」ですが、「ダブル・パッセージ型」よりもさらに読むべき文書量が多く、また Reading Section の最後ということもあってか、とても難しく見え、最初から解くことをあきらめてはいませんか。

　75 分と解答時間の限られた Reading Section ですから、15 問全てを解くとなると、時間が不足するのは仕方のないことかもしれません。しかし、**「トリプル・パッセージ型」は決して「難問」ではないのです。まずは、それぞれのパッセージの「つながり」を意識して読む練習**をしてみましょう（例：求人広告　⇒応募者からのメール　⇒求人側からの結果のお知らせ）。3 つの文書から「ストーリー」が見えてくれば、解ける問題も増えていくはずです。

▶ Part 7 Triple Passages

次の英文を読んで、設問に対する答えとして最も適切なものを選択肢の中から選びましょう。

Wilmslow (January 17) – City officials announced this morning that the Central Museum of Art had been finally completed. Since Wilmslow City started promoting itself as a city of art 10 years ago, building this size of art museum had been its top priority. "However," the then mayor, Catharine McGregor, comments, "We had a serious financial situation at that time and nearly gave up on the plan. Therefore, I am delighted to finally attend the opening ceremony."

　The plan made a great step forward when Simons Digital Co., Ltd. donated land where a factory had been closed in 2013. "We fully agreed on the idea of promoting the city then," says the CEO, Anthony Simon, "and hope the new museum will be a center of collaboration between art and the digital industry."

　The museum will be opening to the public on February 1. To celebrate its opening, local residents will be invited to a series of special events to be held from February 2 to February 4. For further information, please visit the Web site at www.centralart.org.

http://www.xxxx/xxxx/

Opening Events

Day 1 ~ The Local Artists ~
10:00 – 11:30 A.M., The Auditorium
Do you know any artists from our city? Professor Ted Wilson of South Wilmslow University will provide you with a lecture on some of the art works of two locally raised artists, a popular painter and a famous sculptor.

Day 2 ~ Let's Paint Pictures with Mom and Dad! ~
11:00 A.M. – 1:30 P.M (including a 45-minute break for lunch), Studio 201
Children like painting pictures much more than you think they do. In this seminar, professional painters will demonstrate some easy and effective ways to create great art. Registration is limited to 20 pairs (pair = one parent and one child).

Day 3 ~ The World of Auctions ~
1:00 – 3:00 P.M, Lecture Room 3
Aren't you interested in how art dealers price artworks? Ms. Elly Cheng, one of the top art dealers in this country, will tell you some of the secrets she uses to evaluate artwork.

Note:
*Attending the event on Day 2 costs $10 for painting materials. The other events are free of charge.
*Online reservations must be made beforehand to participate in the events. Please e-mail events@ centralart.org to let us know your contact details, the number of participants and the event you would like to attend.

To: events@centralart.org
From: Brian Kim <briankim@eplus.net>
Date: January 20
Subject: Event participation

Dear Sir / Madam,

I am writing to inquire about the event to be held on Day 2. I would like to attend it with my twin children, and am wondering if I could participate with both of them as one pair. Unfortunately, my wife can't come as she will be on a business trip. I would be grateful if you could let me take both of my children to the event.

I look forward to hearing from you.

Best regards,
Brian

Q21. Who is Anthony Simon?

    (A) A city official   (B) A museum director

    (C) An IT engineer   (D) A company executive

Q22. What is mentioned about Wilmslow City?

    (A) It subsidized a local company.

    (B) It suffered from some financial problems.

    (C) It has a plan to renovate the museum.

    (D) It is promoting the arts industry.

Q23. When will the lecture be given?

    (A) On February 1   (B) On February 2

    (C) On February 3   (D) On February 4

Q24. What will most likely happen to Brian Kim when he attends the event?

    (A) He will need to pay an extra fee.

    (B) He will have a chance to make a sculpture.

    (C) He will have to contact his wife.

    (D) He will be offered a free meal for lunch.

Q25. Who is NOT scheduled to join any of the events?

    (A) Catharine McGregor   (B) Anthony Simon

    (C) Ted Wilson   (D) Elly Cheng

▶ ボキャブラリーアルファ 7 Sports/Health

この章のトピックでよく出る単語と表現です。日本語訳を見ながら英単語を声に出して言ってみましょう。

●スポーツ / 健康のトピックに出てくる単語　　CD 2-14

1 ☐ **admit** [ədmít]	動	認める
2 ☐ **potential** [pəténʃ(ə)l]	名	潜在能力
3 ☐ **allow** [əláu]	動	許す
4 ☐ **habit** [hǽbit]	名	習慣
5 ☐ **effective** [iféktiv]	形	効果的な
6 ☐ **temperature** [témpə(r)tʃùə(r)]	名	体温、温度
7 ☐ **interaction** [ìntərǽkʃ(ə)n]	名	対話、相互作用
8 ☐ **monitor** [mánətə(r)]	動	監視する、観察する
9 ☐ **range** [réin(d)ʒ]	名	範囲
10 ☐ **jump** [dʒʌ́mp]	動	飛ぶ、跳ねる
11 ☐ **annually** [ǽnju(ə)li]	副	毎年、年々
12 ☐ **reconcile** [rék(ə)nsàil]	動	仲直りさせる、調和させる
13 ☐ **ache** [éik]	名	痛み
14 ☐ **disperse** [dispə́:(r)s]	動	散らす
15 ☐ **borrow** [bárou]	動	借りる
16 ☐ **obesity** [oubí:səti]	名	肥満
17 ☐ **assessment** [əsésmənt]	名	見積もり、評価
18 ☐ **instrument** [ínstrəmənt]	名	道具、器具
19 ☐ **dose** [dóus]	名	(薬の) 一服
20 ☐ **continue** [kəntínju:]	動	続ける

●スポーツ / 健康のトピックに出てくる表現　　CD 2-15

21 ☐ **take back**	取り戻す、返品する
22 ☐ **build up**	積み重ねる
23 ☐ **spectator sport**	見るスポーツ
24 ☐ **track and field**	陸上競技
25 ☐ **shoulder blade**	肩甲骨
26 ☐ **martial art**	格闘技
27 ☐ **breast stroke**	平泳ぎ
28 ☐ **ball park**	野球場
29 ☐ **locker room**	更衣室
30 ☐ **golf driving range**	ゴルフ練習場

Memo

....

....

....

....

....

....

....

....

....

....

UNIT 8 Doctor's Office / Pharmacy

▶ Key Vocabulary

CD 2-16

この章に出てくる下の英単語の中から日本語訳に当てはまる記号を（ ）に記入しましょう。
答え合わせをしたら音声を聞いて英単語を声に出して読み、つづりを書き込み覚えましょう。

●医院 / 薬局のトピックに出てくる単語

1.	聴診器	( )	9.	同僚	( )
2.	議長	( )	10.	申し込み	( )
3.	処方箋	( )	11.	妨害する	( )
4.	時間帯	( )	12.	指定する	( )
5.	割り当てる	( )	13.	遵守する	( )
6.	しるし	( )	14.	変える	( )
7.	便宜を図る	( )	15.	提案	( )
8.	倉庫	( )	16.	感動させる	( )

a. accommodate	**b.** token	**c.** peer	**d.** chairperson
e. observe	**f.** impress	**g.** stethoscope	**h.** suggestion
i. prescription	**j.** assign	**k.** alter	**l.** designate
m. application	**n.** obstruct	**o.** slot	**p.** storage

LISTENING SECTION

Strategy for Part 1 《写真描写問題の解き方》

物の位置関係を見極めよう①

下の Warming-Up の写真を見ながら位置関係が合っているかどうか確認しましょう。

● 前置詞で始まる修飾語句の中でも、位置関係の表現は多く出題されます。基本的な前置詞句 at the shop「店で」、on the wall「壁に」、in the box「箱の中に」、behind the bed「ベッドの後ろで」などは聞いてすぐに位置関係をイメージできるようにしておきましょう。

 Warming-Up CD 2-17

音声を聞いて（　　）内の語を穴埋めし、
正しい答えはどれか選びましょう。

(A) The sales-person is standing behind the
(　　　　　　).
(B) The girl is wearing a (　　　　　　) suit.
(C) There is a clock on the (　　　).
(D) The woman has placed her (　　　) on the
girl's shoulder.　　正しい答え　(A) (B) (C) (D)

73

▶ Part 1 Photographs

英文を聞き、4つの中から最も適切な描写を選びましょう。

Q1.

Ⓐ Ⓑ Ⓒ Ⓓ

Q2.

Ⓐ Ⓑ Ⓒ Ⓓ

Strategy for Part 2 《応答問題の解き方》

提案・勧誘・依頼① Why don't you ～ ?

　Why don't you ～ ? で始まる表現は直訳すると「どうして～しないの？」ですが、要するに「してもよいではないですか？」のニュアンスで、「提案」や「勧誘」を表しています。

Warming-Up  2-20

音声を聞いて、それぞれの疑問文の意味を記入しましょう。

① Why don't you go to the lobby?
（　　　　　　　　　　　　　　　　　　　　　　　　　　　）

② Why don't we talk with the manager?
（　　　　　　　　　　　　　　　　　　　　　　　　　　　）

▶ Part 2 Question-Response

 2-21,22,23,24

設問に対する応答として、最も適切なものを選びましょう。

Q3. Mark your answer on your answer sheet.　　Ⓐ Ⓑ Ⓒ

Q4. Mark your answer on your answer sheet.　　Ⓐ Ⓑ Ⓒ

Q5. Mark your answer on your answer sheet.　　Ⓐ Ⓑ Ⓒ

Q6. Mark your answer on your answer sheet.　　Ⓐ Ⓑ Ⓒ

Strategy for Part 3 ≪会話問題の解き方≫

図表を含む問題②　設問は説明される順番と同じ？

　Part 3, Part 4 では、音声の流れる順番にヒントが出てくることが多いので、設問はほぼ最初の問題から順番に解くことができます。しかし**図表に関しては音声を聞く前に何に気を付けて聞くべきか、予測する必要があります。**

🌀 Warming-Up

下の Part 3 の問題の図表をみて、図表に何が書いてあるのか答えましょう。
Dr. Daniels のスケジュールで、左の欄と真ん中の欄にはそれぞれ
（　　　　　　　　　　）と（　　　　　　　　　　　　）が書いてあり、右の欄には患者の名前
が書いてある。

▶ Part 3 Short Conversation

 2-25,26

会話文を聞いて、各設問に対する最も適切な答えを 4 つの選択肢から選びましょう。

Dr. Daniels	Time	Client's name
Tuesday	10:00 A.M.	Ms. Stacy Robbins
Tuesday	1:00 P.M.	（　　　　　　　）
Friday	10:00 A.M.	Mr. Powell
Friday	1:00 P.M.	（　　　　　　　）

Q7. Look at the chart. Which time slot was the caller originally assigned to?

(A) Tuesday morning　　　　　　(B) Tuesday afternoon

(C) Friday morning　　　　　　　(D) Friday afternoon

Q8. What is the purpose of the conversation?

(A) To plan a business trip　　　(B) To greet each other

(C) To prepare for meal　　　　　(D) To reschedule the visit

Q9. Why will the woman be out of town on Tuesday?

(A) She will be on traveling for work.　　(B) She will go back home.

(C) She will visit her friend.　　　　　　(D) She will go sightseeing.

トークの「展開」はほぼ決まっている！⑥

　Part 4 でよく登場するトークに「**留守番電話のメッセージ (telephone message)**」があります。聞き手が後でメッセージを聞く際、どんな情報が必要かを考えましょう。すると、この種類のトークの典型的な展開が見えてきます。まず、「**名乗る**」、次に「**電話の目的**」を知らせる…となりませんか。

🔵 Warming-Up 💿 2-27

次の、説明文に入る前の音声を、スクリプトを見ながら聞きましょう。

「音声スクリプト」 "Questions 10 through 12 refer to the following telephone message."
この音声が聞こえ、設問に "Why is the speaker calling?" とある場合、「話し手が
（　叫んでいる・電話している・呼んでいる　）理由」が問われています。正しいものを
1つ選び、○で囲みましょう。

▶ Part 4　Short Talk

説明文を聞いて、各設問に対する最も適切な答えを4つの選択肢から選びましょう。

Q10. Why is the speaker calling?

    (A) To apologize for her mistake

    (B) To report on a medical problem

    (C) To confirm an event venue

    (D) To reschedule an appointment

Q11. What is most likely available on the Web site?

    (A) The clinic's booking status

    (B) Dr. Lindsey's schedule

    (C) An instruction manual

    (D) A timetable for an event

Q12. What is the listener asked to do?

    (A) Contact the reception

    (B) Attend a conference

    (C) Use the online system

    (D) Leave a message

READING SECTION

Strategy for Part 5　《短文穴埋め問題のための Grammar》

文法問題①　接続詞の種類と接続詞ではない「接続副詞」
....
☆**接続詞の基本ルール**

　S＋V のかたまりを含む文を「**節**」と言います。英語の文章ではこの「**節**」が１文（大文字で始まってピリオドで終わるまで）**で２つ以上あったら接続詞でつながなければいけません。**

☆「**等位接続詞**」と「**従属接続詞**」

　接続詞には大きく分けて「**等位接続詞**」と「**従属接続詞（従位接続詞ともいう）**」があります。

　「**等位接続詞**」は「**節**」と「**節**」、「**句**」と「**句**」、「**語**」と「**語**」を**対等に結びつけます。**
for, and, nor, but, or, yet, so などがあります。

　I can speak <u>English</u> **and** <u>French</u>.（私は英語とフランス語を話すことができます。）
　　　　　　　　　　対等(語と語)

「**従属接続詞**」は「**節**」と「**節**」を結びますが、**接続詞のある節が、従属節**（時、理由、条件を表す）、**接続詞のない節が主節**、というように「**差**」をつけて結びます。

　時を表す when, while, as, after, before, since

　原因目的を表す because, as, so that, now that

　条件、譲歩のかたまりを作る if, unless, in case, although, though
などがあります。

　I like Betty **because** she is kind.（私はベティーが好きです、なぜなら彼女は優しいからです。）
　　〈主節〉　　なぜなら　〈従属節〉理由を表しています。

☆**接続詞ではない「接続副詞」！**

　「**接続詞**」と似たような意味があり、役割も似ている「**接続副詞**」がありますが、「**接続詞**」**ではありません。**

　Otherwise（さもないと）、however（しかしながら）、therefore（それゆえに）、furthermore（さらに）、moreover（その上）、nevertheless（それにもかかわらず）などがあります。

特徴①　節と節を結びつけることはできない。

　× I was very sad, **therefore** I went out.

特徴②　セミコロンの直後に用いれば、接続詞のように節と節を結びつけることができる。

　　　（セミコロン自体に文を結びつける機能があるからです。）

　◎ I was very sad**; therefore,** I went out.

　　（私はとても悲しかった。それゆえに、出て行った。）

次の接続副詞の意味を下から選んで記号を（　　）内に記入しましょう。
   (1) consequently   (　　)   **(2)** in addition   (　　)
   (3) meanwhile   (　　)   **(4)** still   (　　)
   (5) afterward   (　　)

   a. それでもなお   **b.** その上   **c.** その後   **d.** その結果   **e.** その一方で

▶ Part 5　Incomplete Sentences

空所に入る最も適切な語句を選びましょう。

Q13. Donations will be used to support the company's museums (　　) the recreational center.
   (A) moreover   (B) and   (C) when   (D) so

Q14. Instructors at Wales Cycling Academy will be using the storage room as their office (　　) the renovation period.
   (A) whereas   (B) when   (C) because   (D) during

Q15. Doctors at Rosemary Memorial Clinic have to submit their peer evaluations (　　) the last day of this month.
   (A) through   (B) right   (C) before   (D) beyond

Q16. The managers will start choosing new accounting staff (　　) the application deadline has passed.
   (A) now that   (B) however   (C) nor   (D) right away

Strategy for Part 6　≪長文穴埋め問題の解き方≫

文法①
　「TOEIC L&R で必要とされる文法はどのレベルだろう？」という疑問を持ったことはありませんか。確かに Reading Section、特に Part 5 と Part 6 では一定の文法力が必要です。しかし残念ながら、「中学や高校で習った英文法をほとんど覚えていない」という理由で、TOEIC L&R にも苦手意識を持ってしまう人も少なくないようです。
　結論として、TOEIC L&R では**「中学校で学ぶレベルの英文法は必須」**となります。ちなみに文法力は、皆さんの「敵」ではなく「味方」になってくれます。遠回りに思えるかもしれませんが、一定レベルの文法を身に着けておいた方が、**後々スコアの伸びが速くなります**。夏休みや春休みなど、まとまった時間に、中学英文法の問題集を一冊終わらせてみてはいかがでしょう。あの頃理解できなかった文法が、今ではよく理解できることに気づくかもしれませんよ。

▶ Part 6 Text Completion

次の英文を読んで、選択肢の中から空所に入る最も適切な語句を選びましょう。

Parking Rules

Sainsbury Hospital would like to ask visitors to ------- the rules about parking.
17.
Recently, we have received many complaints about vehicles which are illegally
parked in the neighborhood. ------- . It will not only trouble the neighbors, but
18.
also obstruct the ambulances coming in and out. If we find any cars parked
along the roads, the drivers will be fined $300. We have two designated parking
areas nearby. One is just behind the East Building, and the other is ------- a
19.
three-minute walk from the West Building. They can accommodate 200 cars in
total. Please make sure to get your carpark ticket ------- at the reception and
20.
your parking will be free.

Thank you for your cooperation.
The Director of Sainsbury Hospital

Q17. (A) observe   (B) apply   (C) alter   (D) protect

Q18. (A) Security cameras are in operation 24 hours a day.
     (B) Making a lot of noise may disturb the neighbors.
     (C) Dealing with the complaints is time-consuming for the staff.
     (D) Please do not park any vehicles on the roads around the hospital.

Q19. (A) onto   (B) by   (C) within   (D) along

Q20. (A) stamped   (B) stamping   (C) stamps   (D) stamp

Strategy for Part 7 ≪読解問題の解き方≫

設問パターン④

Unit 2 で紹介した Part 7 の設問の種類のうち、「3. 書き手の意図を推測するパター
ン（通称・意図問題）」について説明します。

Part 7 の**全 54 問中 2 問**しか出題されないこのパターンの設問ですが、必ず「テキス
トメッセージ」や「チャット」といった文章について出題されます。「What does the
writer mean when he / she writes, "～～～"?」のような形で、チャット内の特定
の文が引用され、その発言の意図を問われます。

実際に皆さんがチャットで文を入力する際、関連する内容はどこに書かれていますか
…その文の前ですよね。そして、チャットでも必ず「ストーリー」があります。「流れ」
をとらえ、その文の前後の文に注意すれば、おのずと正解は選べます。

次の英文を読んで、設問に対する答えとして最も適切なものを選択肢の中から選びましょう。

Chat Telephone

▶ Margaret May (10:10 A.M.)
Good morning Edward and Thomas. How did you find your observation at Mount Hospital yesterday?

▶ Edward McNeil (10:11 A.M.)
Hi Margaret. Sorry I couldn't make much time to talk to you on the phone from the hospital.

▶ Thomas Sinclair (10:11 A.M.)
Hello Margaret. Yes, the staff members at the hospital who showed us around were so kind, and they introduced us to many of the doctors and nurses working there.

▶ Edward McNeil (10:12 A.M.)
And they gave us many suggestions on how to build our new clinic, right? How are you doing, Margaret?

▶ Margaret May (10:14 A.M.)
I wish I could have gone with you. I'm too busy seeing my patients and doing the paperwork we need to submit to city hall right now. So, tell me what you found at Mount Hospital.

▶ Thomas Sinclair (10:15 A.M.)
Sorry, we left all of that work to you. I was impressed with, for example, the wooden balcony on the rooftop.

▶ Edward McNeil (10:16 A.M.)
Agree. The patients and the staff seemed very relaxed there. Something similar would be good for our clinic.

▶ Margaret May (10:17 A.M.)
Sounds brilliant. I'll ask the constructor for an estimate. Anything I can do now?

▶ Thomas Sinclair (10:19 A.M.)
Thanks but there are too many things to discuss with you. I'll come to your office later to tell you about the ideas we may be able to apply to our own clinic.

▶ Edward McNeil (10:20 A.M.)
I'll be joining you two around noon. See you then.

Q21. What is most likely true about Ms. May?
(A) She sent out some documents to the city office.
(B) She visited Mount Hospital with her friends.
(C) She will become a medical doctor soon.
(D) She will establish a clinic with her colleagues.

Q22. What is indicated about Mr. McNeil?
(A) He used to be a medical doctor.
(B) He made a call to Ms. May at the hospital.
(C) He has not seen Mr. Sinclair before.
(D) He has to submit some reports.

Q23. What is suggested about Mount Hospital?
(A) It has been recently completed.
(B) It has an open space for relaxing.
(C) It is scheduled to be relocated.
(D) It is supposed to hire additional doctors.

Q24. At 10:17 A.M., what does Ms. May most likely mean when she writes, "Sounds brilliant"?
(A) She is willing to help her colleagues.
(B) She agrees with Mr. McNeil on his budget plan.
(C) She shows an interest in her co-workers' idea.
(D) She evaluates Mount Hospital's policy highly.

Q25. What will Ms. May most likely do next?
(A) Sign a contract
(B) Make an appointment
(C) Contact a builder
(D) Give an estimate

この章のトピックでよく出る単語と表現です。日本語訳を見ながら英単語を声に出して言ってみましょう。

●医院 / 薬局のトピックに出てくる単語 🎧 2-30

1 ☐ **vaccination** [vǽksənèiʃən]	名	予防接種
2 ☐ **hospitalization** [hɑ́spitəlaizéiʃən]	名	入院
3 ☐ **diagnose** [dáiəgnòus]	動	診断する
4 ☐ **appointment** [əpɔ́intmənt]	名	予約
5 ☐ **ambulance** [ǽmbjələns]	名	救急車
6 ☐ **investigate** [invéstəgèit]	動	精査する、調査する
7 ☐ **incur** [inkə́:(r)]	動	こうむる
8 ☐ **infectious** [infékʃəs]	形	伝染性の
9 ☐ **method** [méθəd]	名	方法、方式
10 ☐ **commit** [kəmít]	動	委託する、身をゆだねる
11 ☐ **garment** [gá:(r)mənt]	名	衣類
12 ☐ **control** [kəntróul]	名	支配、管理
13 ☐ **cavity** [kǽvəti]	名	虫歯
14 ☐ **recommendation** [rèkəməndéiʃən]	名	勧告、推薦
15 ☐ **accumulate** [əkjú:mjəlèit]	動	累積する
16 ☐ **prevention** [privénʃən]	名	予防
17 ☐ **sample** [sǽmpl]	名	サンプル、見本
18 ☐ **conservative** [kənsá:(r)vətiv]	形	保守的な
19 ☐ **cure** [kjúə(r)]	動	治す、治療する
20 ☐ **experiment** [ikspérəmənt]	名	実験

●医院 / 薬局のトピックに出てくる表現 🎧 2-31

21 ☐ **fill out**	記入する
22 ☐ **critical condition**	重篤な状態
23 ☐ **side effect**	副作用
24 ☐ **dietary fiber**	食物繊維
25 ☐ **over-the-counter**	市販の、処方箋なしで買える
26 ☐ **incubation period**	潜伏期
27 ☐ **sore throat**	喉の痛み
28 ☐ **runny nose**	鼻水
29 ☐ **medical diagnosis**	医学的診断
30 ☐ **generic drug**	商標未登録の薬

UNIT 9　Hobbies / Art

▶ Key Vocabulary
 2-32

この章に出てくる下の英単語の中から日本語訳に当てはまる記号を（　）に記入しましょう。
答え合わせをしたら音声を聞いて英単語を声に出して読み、つづりを書き込み覚えましょう。

●趣味 / 芸術のトピックに出てくる単語

1.	漕ぐ	（　　）	9.	～に代わって	（　　）
2.	拍手する	（　　）	10.	中間の	（　　）
3.	観客	（　　）	11.	置く	（　　）
4.	失効する	（　　）	12.	入会する	（　　）
5.	制作室	（　　）	13.	熱望して	（　　）
6.	続く	（　　）	14.	免除する	（　　）
7.	減少する	（　　）	15.	入会	（　　）
8.	～にかかわらず	（　　）	16.	授業料	（　　）

- **a.** last
- **b.** regardless of
- **c.** eager
- **d.** row
- **e.** place
- **f.** exempt
- **g.** on behalf of
- **h.** admission
- **i.** expire
- **j.** applaud
- **k.** tuition
- **l.** studio
- **m.** intermediate
- **n.** enroll
- **o.** spectator
- **p.** decline

LISTENING SECTION

Strategy for Part 1　《写真描写問題の解き方》

動詞の時制は何？

下の Warming-Up の写真を見ながらいつのことについて言っているか考えましょう。

● Part 1 は「写真描写問題」であり、基本的に一枚の写真で表現できる時制は「現在」であることがほとんどです。正解の選択肢の多くが「現在進行形」や「現在形」ですが、未来を表す be about to や、完了形が正解になることもあります。

 Warming-Up　2-33

音声を聞いて（　　　）内の語を穴埋めし、
正しい答えはどれか選びましょう。

(A) People are (　　　　　) in the semi-finals.
(B) A woman is (　　　　　) a racket.
(C) A boy is (　　　） to hit the ball.
(D) The game was (　　　　　) in the
　　　 morning.　　　 正しい答え　(A) (B) (C) (D)

▶ Part 1 Photographs

英文を聞き、4つの中から最も適切な描写を選びましょう。

Q1.

(A) (B) (C) (D)

Q2.

(A) (B) (C) (D)

Strategy for Part 2 ≪応答問題の解き方≫

提案・勧誘・依頼② Could you ～? Can you ～?

Could you ～? Can you ～? で始まる表現は直訳すると「～できましたか？」「～できますか？」ですが、「～していただけますか？」のニュアンスで、「依頼」や「提案」も表しています。

● Warming-Up 🅒🅓 2-36

音声を聞いて、それぞれの疑問文の意味を記入しましょう。

① Could you prepare for the festival?

(   )

② Can you tell me who he is?

(   )

▶ Part 2 Question-Response

設問に対する応答として、最も適切なものを選びましょう。

Q3. Mark your answer on your answer sheet.   (A) (B) (C)

Q4. Mark your answer on your answer sheet.   (A) (B) (C)

Q5. Mark your answer on your answer sheet.   (A) (B) (C)

Q6. Mark your answer on your answer sheet.   (A) (B) (C)

Strategy for Part 3 ≪会話問題の解き方≫

3人の会話問題② 「どんなつもりで言ったの？」と意図を問う問題

Part 3, Part 4 では、話し手の意図を問う問題が出題されます。

当然、設問にある会話部分だけを聞くのではなく、全体像を把握し、英文の意味を正確にとることが必要です。

⬤ Warming-Up

次の設問の日本語訳を書きましょう。

What does the woman mean when she says, "I understand him." ?

( )

▶ Part 3 Short Conversation

 2-41,42

会話文を聞いて、各設問に対する最も適切な答えを4つの選択肢から選びましょう。

Q7. Where does the conversation probably take place?

    (A) In an office building   (B) In the theater

    (C) In an airport   (D) In a cafeteria

Q8. What does Grace imply when she says, "Well, I've left my computer in my office downstairs"?

    (A) The computer is broken.   (B) She doesn't want to drink coffee.

    (C) The theater is too far away.   (D) She wants to check the website.

Q9. What kind of movie are the speakers considering?

    (A) Horror   (B) Science fiction

    (C) Romance   (D) Comedy

「言い換え」の選択肢

　TOEIC L&R では、リスニング問題・リーディング問題共に、**語句**の「**言い換え (paraphrase) 力**」が問われます。Part 4 でも、トークで聞こえるヒントが、同じ語句を使った正解選択肢になっていないケースも多く見られます。例えば、リスニング中に「a mechanical trouble」と聞こえたのに、正解選択肢では「a technical problem」となっていたりします。また、一概には言えませんが、トークの中で目立って聞こえた語句をそのまま使っている選択肢は、**誤りを誘う「誤答選択肢 (distracter)」**であることも少なくありません。

Warming-Up 💿2-43

次の音声を言い換えた語句は何ですか。正しいものを1つ選び、○で囲み、完成させましょう。
「音声スクリプト」"Send an e-mail to a colleague"
⇒ Contact a (coworker / client / customer / supplier)

▶ Part 4 Short Talk

 2-44,45

説明文を聞いて、各設問に対する最も適切な答えを4つの選択肢から選びましょう。

Q10. When will the event finish?

　　(A) On February 24

　　(B) On February 26

　　(C) On March 3

　　(D) On March 17

Q11. Who is Kate Williams?

　　(A) An artist

　　(B) A printer

　　(C) A reporter

　　(D) A professor

Q12. According to the speaker, what will James Honobe do?

　　(A) Give away a copy of his book

　　(B) Explain details of the artwork

　　(C) Introduce a history of the museum

　　(D) Present information on future events

READING SECTION

Strategy for Part 5 《短文穴埋め問題のための Grammar 》

文法問題② 接続詞 vs 前置詞のよくあるパターンと相関語句

選択肢に前置詞、接続副詞、接続詞が並ぶ、「**接続詞**」VS「**前置詞**」の問題は Part 5 で頻出します。

☆**接続詞と前置詞の見分け方**

接続詞：接続詞の後ろには **S+V** のかたまりである「節」がきます。

前置詞：前置詞の後に続くのは必ず「**名詞**」もしくは「**名詞相当語句**」です。

接続詞 VS 前置詞の典型例
Part 5 でよく出題される識別

接続詞	前置詞句	
because	because of ～	「～なので」
while	during	「～のあいだ」
since	due to	「～の理由で」
although	despite	「～にもかかわらず」
unless	without	「～がなければ」

空所の後が、名詞句なのか、節なのかを見て、空所に入れる語や品詞を選びましょう。

☆**相関語句のパターン**

接続語句の組み合わせの「**相関語句**」はよく出題されるので「決まり文句」として試験直前にも見直しておきましょう。

☐ both A and B 「A も B もどちらも」
☐ either A or B 「A か B のどちらか」
☐ not only A but (also) B 「A だけでなく B もまた」
☐ A as well as B 「B だけでなく A も」
☐ not A but B 「A ではなく B」
☐ neither A nor B 「A も B も～ない」

● Warming-Up

次の相関語句を含む文の日本語訳を書きましょう。

(1) Neither his mother nor his father speaks French.

（　　　　　　　　　　　　　　　　　　　　　　　　）

(2) A messy refrigerator is both unprofessional and unsanitary.

（　　　　　　　　　　　　　　　　　　　　　　　　）

(3) Not only was the chair delivered 30 days late, but it was also broken.

（　　　　　　　　　　　　　　　　　　　　　　　　）

▶ Part 5 Incomplete Sentences

空所に入る最も適切な語句を選びましょう。

Q13. Breakfast will be served until 10:00 (   ) supplies last.

    (A) before   (B) after   (C) while   (D) when

Q14. (   ) making several unsuccessful phone calls, the patient decided to visit the clinic.

    (A) Although   (B) But   (C) Because   (D) After

Q15. You should choose the credit card payment option for your order (   ) we don't accept payment upon delivery.

    (A) as   (B) once   (C) either   (D) besides

Q16. (   ) the fact that the number of mobile phones is increasing, time spent talking on the phone is significantly declining.

    (A) However   (B) Although   (C) In spite of   (D) But

....

Strategy for Part 6 《長文穴埋め問題の解き方》

語彙の増やし方①

    Unit 7 で紹介した Part 6 の設問の種類のうち、「2. 文脈に沿って解く問題」のうちの「語彙を選ぶ問題（通称・語彙問題）」について説明します。

    TOEIC L&R の Part 6 全 **16** 問中、**2 ～ 4** 問程度出題される「語彙問題」では、文脈も考えた上で最もふさわしい単語を選びます。よって、空欄の前後との関係が重要になります。そこで、例えば動詞を覚える際、「動詞＋目的語」のように「**フレーズ（語句のかたまり）で覚える**」習慣をつけることをお勧めします。その単語だけ単独で覚えるよりも記憶に残る方法であり、かつ、単語はその「意味」と同様に「使い方」も大切なのです。

▶ Part 6 Text Completion

次の英文を読んで、選択肢の中から空所に入る最も適切な語句を選びましょう。

East Town New Year's Festival

We are pleased to announce that the New Year's festival will be held on New Year's Eve as scheduled. In this severe recession, it was hard to raise funds for the festival. ------- 17. . Without their cooperation, we could not have the festival this year. ------- 18. local citizens, we express our deepest gratitude to them. This year, there will be special performances by some famous musicians on the stage, ------- 19. is to be set in the center of the venue. Further information is now available on this Web site. We look forward to ------- 20. the New Year with you.

Q17. (A) Therefore, we cannot expect many tourists to come.

(B) Accordingly, there will be fewer street stalls this year.

(C) Meanwhile, we had to reduce the number of guests.

(D) However, some companies offered to support us.

Q18. (A) Despite of   (B) Regardless of

(C) On behalf of   (D) Either of

Q19. (A) what   (B) which

(C) who   (D) where

Q20. (A) be celebrated   (B) celebrating

(C) have celebrated   (D) be celebrating

設問パターン⑤

Unit 2 で紹介した Part 7 の設問の種類のうち、「**4. 単語の意味を問うパターン（通称・同義語問題）**」について説明します。

Part 7 の**全 54 問中、多くて 5 問程度**は出題されます。問われている語がある場所は「○段落・×行目」のように明記されており、解答にあまり時間はかかりません。よって、このタイプの問題は、**テストの残り時間が少ない時でも必ず解く**ことをお勧めします。その際、仮に単語の意味を知っていたとしても、果たしてその意味が文脈に当てはまるかどうかまで確認してください。

この Unit の Part 6 の Strategy で触れた「語彙の増やし方」ですが、新しい単語を覚える際には、類義語もチェックし、まとめて覚えることも有効な方法です。

▶ Part 7 Single Passage

次の英文を読んで、設問に対する答えとして最も適切なものを選択肢の中から選びましょう。

Roy's Guitar School Opening New Courses

Do you want to play your favorite songs? If so, why don't you join us?
Roy's Guitar School will be opening our new teaching studio here in Altrincham
at the beginning of July. The studio will have the most up-to-date equipment.
There will be three courses offered, Introductory, Intermediate and Advanced,
by our fabulous instructors. Students will be placed according to their level of
guitar skills. To enroll, please fill out the application form below:

Name: *Peter Miller*

Age: *41*

Address: *113 Upper Street, Altrincham*

Zip Code: *94043 - 5510*

Phone number: (Home) *555 – 0117*   (Mobile) *0991 - 00417*

E-mail address: *petermiller@appletree.net*

Preferred Course: *Intermediate*

Playing Career: *I played the guitar when I was a high school student but have not played it for a long time. I have an electric guitar, that is now stored, somewhere in my garage. Recently, my friend asked me to join his band, and I've become eager to play the guitar again.*

To celebrate the opening, new students are exempted from the admission fee. **Please send your completed form to us online at roysguitar@networld.com or by fax to 555-2121.** When we decide which course will be best for you, we will e-mail you further information about tuition fees, our bank transfers and schedule. Thank you.

Q21. What is true about Roy's Guitar School?
(A) It has recently opened.
(B) It has a large number of students.
(C) It has state-of-the-art facilities.
(D) It has a variety of studios.

Q22. What information is NOT required on the form?
(A) Favorite songs
(B) Current address
(C) Postal code
(D) Mobile phone number

Q23. The word "enroll" in paragraph 1, line 6, is closest in meaning to
(A) register   (B) hire
(C) appoint   (D) assign

Q24. What will Roy's Guitar School most likely do for Mr. Miller next?
(A) Decide his class
(B) Introduce him one of the instructors
(C) Send him an invoice
(D) Prepare for the welcoming event

Q25. What is suggested about Mr. Miller?
(A) He often plays his electric guitar.
(B) He has a long career as a professional musician.
(C) He has applied for the position of instructor.
(D) He lives in the same town as the school.

▶ ボキャブラリーアルファ 9 Hobbies / Art

この章のトピックでよく出る単語と表現です。日本語訳を見ながら英単語を声に出して言ってみましょう。

● 趣味 / 芸術のトピックに出てくる単語

CD 2-46

1 ☐ **premiere** [primíə(r)]	名	封切り、初公演
2 ☐ **distraction** [distrǽkʃ(ə)n]	名	気晴らし
3 ☐ **aware** [əwéə(r)]	形	気づいている
4 ☐ **criticism** [krítəsìzm]	名	批判
5 ☐ **virtuoso** [və̀:rtʃuóusou]	名	巨匠
6 ☐ **overture** [óuvə(r)tʃùə(r)]	名	序曲
7 ☐ **embroidery** [imbrɔ́id(ə)ri]	名	刺繍
8 ☐ **contemporary** [kəntémpərèri]	形	現代の
9 ☐ **specialize** [spéʃəlàiz]	動	〜を特殊化する、専門化する
10 ☐ **collection** [kəlékʃən]	名	コレクション、収集
11 ☐ **creative** [kriéitiv]	形	創造的な
12 ☐ **calligraphy** [kəlígrəfi]	名	書道
13 ☐ **representation** [rèprizentéiʃən]	名	表現、代表
14 ☐ **eclectic** [ikléktik]	形	折衷的な
15 ☐ **express** [iksprés]	動	表現する
16 ☐ **multiplex** [mʌ́ltəplèks]	名	シネコン（複合型映画館）
17 ☐ **blockbuster** [blákbʌ́stər]	名	大ヒット作
18 ☐ **matinee** [mæt(ə)néi]	名	昼興行

● 趣味 / 芸術のトピックに出てくる表現

CD 2-47

19 ☐ **revolving stage**	（演劇の）回り舞台
20 ☐ **box office**	チケット売り場
21 ☐ **law enforcement**	法の執行
22 ☐ **give up**	あきらめる、やめる
23 ☐ **pull out**	手を引く、参加をやめる
24 ☐ **spare time**	余暇
25 ☐ **on hand**	入手できる
26 ☐ **cultural heritage**	文化遺産
27 ☐ **rain check**	またの誘いを受ける約束
28 ☐ **standing ovation**	大喝采
29 ☐ **amusement park**	遊園地
30 ☐ **intangible cultural asset**	無形文化財

▶ Key Vocabulary

 2-48

この章に出てくる下の英単語の中から日本語訳に当てはまる記号を（　）に記入しましょう。
答え合わせをしたら音声を聞いて英単語を声に出して読み、つづりを書き込み覚えましょう。

● 教育 / 学校のトピックに出てくる単語

1.	うがいをする	（　　）	9.	体育館	（　　）
2.	視覚の	（　　）	10.	平均台	（　　）
3.	延期する	（　　）	11.	適格で	（　　）
4.	パンフレット	（　　）	12.	妨害	（　　）
5.	平面図	（　　）	13.	表面上は	（　　）
6.	幾何学	（　　）	14.	異なる	（　　）
7.	補修的な	（　　）	15.	評価する	（　　）
8.	数学	（　　）	16.	緊急に	（　　）

a. gymnasium	**b.** floor plan	**c.** geometry	**d.** brochure
e. gargle	**f.** vary	**g.** eligible	**h.** measure
i. balance beam	**j.** remedial	**k.** postpone	**l.** interruption
m. optical	**n.** seemingly	**o.** urgently	**p.** mathematics

LISTENING SECTION

Strategy for Part 1 《写真描写問題の解き方》

物の位置関係を見極めよう②
下の Warming-Up の写真を見ながら位置関係が合っているかどうか確認しましょう。

● 前置詞で始まる修飾語句は Unit 8 でふれたもの以外にも under the chair「椅子の下に」、across the street「道の向かい側に」、along the shore「海岸に沿って」などが多く出題されます。また、状況を表す in a row「一列に、続けて」、side by side「並んで」なども覚えておきましょう。

Warming-Up 2-49

音声を聞いて（　　）内の語を穴埋めし、
正しい答えはどれか選びましょう。

(A) They are sitting (　　　　　　　　　　　　　). （3 語）
(B) The students are talking to (　　　　　　　　).
　　（2 語）
(C) They are singing in a (　　　　). （1 語）
(D) The instructor is looking into the (　　　　　　).
　　（1 語）　　　　　　　正しい答え　(A) (B) (C) (D)

▶ Part 1 Photographs

英文を聞き、4つの中から最も適切な描写を選びましょう。

Q1.

Ⓐ Ⓑ Ⓒ Ⓓ

Q2.

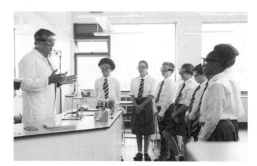

Ⓐ Ⓑ Ⓒ Ⓓ

Strategy for Part 2 ≪応答問題の解き方≫

提案・勧誘・依頼③ Would you mind if ～？

　Would you mind if ～？で始まる表現は、直訳すると「もし～したらあなたは気にしますか？」ですが、「～が～してもいいですか？」のニュアンスで、「許可」や「依頼」などを表しています。「大丈夫です」というつもりで Yes などと答えると「はい、気にします」の意味になってしまいます。気にしない場合は No で始まる表現などが適切です。

🍑 Warming-Up 2-52

音声を聞いて、それぞれの疑問文の意味を記入しましょう。

① Would you mind if I listened to some music?
　(　　　　　　　　　　　　　　　　　　　　　　　　　　　　　　　)
② Would you mind if I opened the door?
　(　　　　　　　　　　　　　　　　　　　　　　　　　　　　　　　)

▶ Part 2 Question-Response

設問に対する応答として、最も適切なものを選びましょう。

Q3. Mark your answer on your answer sheet.　　Ⓐ Ⓑ Ⓒ

Q4. Mark your answer on your answer sheet.　　Ⓐ Ⓑ Ⓒ

Q5. Mark your answer on your answer sheet.　　Ⓐ Ⓑ Ⓒ

Q6. Mark your answer on your answer sheet.　　Ⓐ Ⓑ Ⓒ

Strategy for Part 3 《会話問題の解き方》

3ターンの会話問題②　When を含む設問

　Part 3 の設問のうち、When で始まるのは When is this conversation taking place?「この会話はいつ行われていますか」など会話全体に関する質問であったり、When does the restaurant open?「レストランはいつ開きますか」のような詳細を問う問題であったりします。また、When will the meeting most likely take place?「会議はいつ行われますか」など、第3問目でこれから起こることについて質問することもあります。

⏺ Warming-Up

次の設問を読んで、日本語に訳してから、会話の内容を予測しましょう。

　When will the woman probably eat dinner?

　(　　　　　　　　　　　　　　　　　　　　　　　　　　　　　　　　)

→女性が(　　　　　　　　　　　) を予定しているとわかる。

▶ Part 3　Short Conversation

 2-57,58

会話文を聞いて、各設問に対する最も適切な答えを4つの選択肢から選びましょう。

Q7. Where do the speakers most likely work?

　(A) At a high school　　　　　　(B) At a government agency

　(C) At a remedial school　　　　(D) At a university

Q8. When is this conversation probably taking place?

　(A) At the beginning of summer　(B) In late summer

　(C) In the middle of winter　　　(D) In late winter

Q9. According to the woman, what is her specialization?

　(A) Geology　　　　　　　　　　(B) Mathematics

　(C) Business management　　　　(D) History

トークの「展開」はほぼ決まっている！⑦

　Part 4 で登場するトークに「**留守番電話の自動応答メッセージ（recorded message）**」があります。このメッセージは、通常どのような状況で耳にするでしょうか。考えられるケースとして、「事業所が閉まっている（不在）」、「自動音声での受付ダイヤル」の2つが挙げられます。よって、内容は非常に限定されるのではないでしょうか。

　しかし、油断大敵、**トークを聞く前から「～だ」という決めつけをしてしまうことは危険**です。内容の「想定」は大切ですが、「思い込み」はしないように。

⚲ Warming-Up 🎧2-59

次の、説明文に入る前の音声を、スクリプトを見ながら聞きましょう。

「音声スクリプト」"Questions 10 through 12 refer to the following recorded message."

この音声が聞こえた場合、トーク内で想定される内容を3つ選び、○で囲みましょう。

（答え：「こちらは××です」・「△△様でしょうか」・「（～のため）不在です」・

「（ご用のある方は）～してください」）

▶ Part 4 Short Talk

 2-60,61

説明文を聞いて、各設問に対する最も適切な答えを4つの選択肢から選びましょう。

Q10. What recently happened to Sheffield Language School?

　　(A) It was awarded a prize.

　　(B) It was refurbished.

　　(C) It changed its business hours.

　　(D) It hired more teachers.

Q11. What information is required to book a lesson?

　　(A) An e-mail address

　　(B) A phone number

　　(C) A password

　　(D) An ID number

Q12. Who will contact the listeners if they leave a message?

　　(A) A teacher

　　(B) A constructor

　　(C) A staff member

　　(D) A building manager

READING SECTION

Strategy for Part 5　≪短文穴埋め問題のための Grammar ≫

文法問題③　「関係代名詞」と「関係副詞」

　Part 5 には「関係代名詞」と「関係副詞」の両方が並ぶ問題がよく出題されます。
関係代名詞は「接続詞」と「代名詞」両方の働きをします。
関係副詞は「接続詞」と「副詞」両方の働きをします。

☆「**関係代名詞**」をおさらいしよう

関係代名詞は「接続詞」と同じように、**2 つの文をつないで 1 つの文にする働き**があり、
「（代）名詞」のように、関係代名詞が導く節の中で主語や目的語になります。

先行詞	主格	所有格	目的格
人	who	whose	whom
事物	which	whose	which
人・事物	that	－	that

☆「**関係副詞**」って何？

関係副詞は「接続詞」と同じように **2 つの文をつないで 1 つの文にする働き**があり、**関係副詞が導く節の中で、「副詞」の役割**をします。関係副詞は単なる副詞と考えることもできるため、関係副詞の後に続く文だけで文として成立します。また先行詞は省略することができます。

関係副詞		先行詞の例（省略できる）
時 when	the time, the day	The manager wants to know（the time）**when** you will come.
場所 where	the place, the house	The airport was（the place）**where** I met George.
理由 why	the reason	I don't know（the reason）**why** she is absent today.
方法 how	※ the way	That's **how** they entered the house. = That's **the way** they entered the house.

※the way how ～はありません。（how は先行詞と一緒に用いません）

Warming-Up

関係代名詞の who, which, what に -ever がついたものを複合関係代名詞と言います。
表の空欄に当てはまる語を記入しましょう。

	名詞節を作り、 主語・目的語・補語となる	副詞節を作り、 「譲歩」を表す
whoever	…する人は（　　　　　　　　　） （= anyone who）	誰が…しようとも （=no matter who）
whichever	…するものはどちら（どれ）でも （=any one[ones] that）	（　　　　　）を…しようとも （=no matter which）
whatever	…するものは（　　　　　　　　） （=anything that）	何が…しようとも （=no matter what）

▶ Part 5 Incomplete Sentences

空所に入る最も適切な語句を選びましょう。

Q13. I can't find the book (　　) I borrowed.

    (A) where   (B) whose   (C) which   (D) who

Q14. (　　) I saw in the gymnasium was a big balance beam.

    (A) What   (B) Which   (C) When   (D) Who

Q15. (　　) works hard will succeed.

    (A) Whatever   (B) No matter   (C) However   (D) Whoever

Q16. Let me know the date (　　) we have to submit our schedule.

    (A) which   (B) where   (C) when   (D) who

....

Strategy for Part 6 ≪長文穴埋め問題の解き方≫

語彙の増やし方②

　「TOEIC L&R を受験するために、どのくらい単語を知っていればよいですか？」「何かお勧めの単語の覚え方はありますか？」というような質問をよく受けます。

　まず、TOEIC L&R は、リスニング力とリーディング力を測るテストです。つまり「**読めて聴ける」ようになる**ことが大前提になります。多くの大学生と接していて感じるのは、「日本語と英語を『一対一』で覚えているだけ」の人が多い事です。例えば、「schedule＝予定」だけではなく、schedule「予定を立てる（動詞）」、そこから be scheduled to ～、類義語…と覚えることをお勧めします。また、近頃は音声を無料でダウンロードできる教材も多くなっています。スマートフォンなどで**何度も聞く習慣**をつけてみてはいかがでしょうか。

▶ Part 6 Text Completion

次の英文を読んで、選択肢の中から空所に入る最も適切な語句を選びましょう。

Spring Open Language Course

Highland University will offer local residents some special language courses this spring. ----17.---- you live or work in Highland City, you are eligible to attend any of the courses for free. ----18.---- . For example, the Advanced French courses will be given by Professor Harry Elliott, who is an expert in French language and culture. We are sure that his classes will not only deepen your knowledge of the French language ----19.---- introduce you to the wonders of French culture.

For further information, please visit the Web site, www.hiland.ac.uk. Please note that the number of seats in each class is limited. We look forward to your ----20.---- .

Q17. (A) As long as   (B) Unless
(C) Although   (D) Prior to

Q18. (A) Parking space on campus is unavailable.
(B) Each class lasts for an hour and half.
(C) The campus is conveniently located.
(D) We have many experienced faculty members.

Q19. (A) instead of   (B) as well as
(C) but also   (D) ever since

Q20. (A) appreciation   (B) cooperation
(C) interruption   (D) application

設問パターン⑥

Unit 2 で紹介した Part 7 の設問の種類のうち、「5. 文が入る位置を問うパターン（通称・文位置選択問題）」について説明します。

Part 7 の全 54 問中、わずか 2 問です。文書を一通り読み、ストーリーを理解していないと解けません。よってこのタイプの問題は、テストの残り時間が少ない場合には「捨てる（解答を適当にマークして次に進む）」ことをお勧めします。

皆さんは「時間対効果」を考えたことはありますか。つまり、もしこのタイプの問題に固執して数分を費やした場合、実はその数分で解けるはずだったより多くの易しい問題に解答できなくなるのです。Reading Section の **75 分間**で解ける問題の数を**最大化**することがスコアアップにつながります。

▶ Part 7 Single Passage

次の英文を読んで、設問に対する答えとして最も適切なものを選択肢の中から選びましょう。

Memo

From: Alex Peterson, Personnel Department
To: All staff members
Date: October 13
Subject: Placement test

I am delighted to inform you that Morison Business School has received a number of inquiries about our new online business administration courses. Seemingly, some companies are already planning to provide their new recruits with the courses and have already asked us for an estimate. Considering the number of potential students, their level of business management skills will vary. Therefore, why don't we divide the students into five groups according to their level?

In that case, I think we should implement a placement test well before starting the courses to measure their knowledge of business administration. Some of you may be assigned to make questions for the test. Also, having four more groups means that we will need four more corporate instructors.

We have to urgently consider these matters. If you have any ideas, please visit my office or e-mail me at peterson@mbs.com. While I am away from the office on a business trip next week, Ms. White in the personnel department can supply you with further details.

Q21. What is the purpose of the memo?

(A) To call a conference

(B) To announce schedule changes

(C) To update a job opening

(D) To suggest new plans

Q22. The word "implement" in paragraph 2, line 1, is closest in meaning to

(A) conduct   (B) pass

(C) succeed   (D) enforce

Q23. Who most likely is Ms. White?

(A) Mr. Peterson's colleague

(B) Mr. Peterson's client

(C) A corporate instructor

(D) A test supplier

Q24. What are the staff members asked to do?

(A) Recommend someone for a job

(B) Provide their own ideas

(C) Fix an orientation schedule

(D) Submit a document

Q25. What is most likely true about Morison Business School?

(A) It will reduce the number of employees.

(B) It will have more applications than expected.

(C) It is arranging an event for new employees.

(D) It specializes in providing online courses.

ボキャブラリーアルファ 10 Education / Schools

この章のトピックでよく出る単語と表現です。日本語訳を見ながら英単語を声に出して言ってみましょう。

●教育 / 学校のトピックに出てくる単語　　CD 2-62

1 ☐ **transcript** [trǽnskript]	名	成績証明書
2 ☐ **semester** [səméstə(r)]	名	学期
3 ☐ **survey** [sə́(r)vei]	名	調査
4 ☐ **fulfill** [fulfíl]	動	実現する、達成する
5 ☐ **periodically** [pì(ə)riádik(ə)li]	副	定期的に
6 ☐ **logical** [ládʒikəl]	形	論理的な
7 ☐ **degree** [digrí:]	名	学位
8 ☐ **position** [pəzíʃən]	名	位置、立場
9 ☐ **priority** [praió(:)rəti]	名	優先権
10 ☐ **systematically** [sìstəmǽtik(ə)li]	副	組織として、系統だって
11 ☐ **expertise** [èkspə:(r)tí:z]	名	専門知識、技能
12 ☐ **influx** [ínflʌks]	名	流入
13 ☐ **dialogue** [dáiəlò(:)g]	名	会話、対話
14 ☐ **faculty** [fǽk(ə)lti]	名	学部、教授陣
15 ☐ **assignment** [əsáinmənt]	名	宿題、割り当て
16 ☐ **reference** [réf(ə)r(ə)ns]	名	推薦者
17 ☐ **conform** [kənfɔ́:m]	動	遵守する、守る
18 ☐ **principal** [prínsəpl]	名	学長

●教育 / 学校のトピックに出てくる表現　　CD 2-63

19 ☐ catch up with	追いつく
20 ☐ press release	報道発表、プレスリリース
21 ☐ achievement test	学力試験
22 ☐ liberal arts	一般教養科目
23 ☐ social welfare	社会福祉
24 ☐ adhere to	密着する、くっつく
25 ☐ bring up	話を持ち出す
26 ☐ distance learning	通信教育
27 ☐ remedial education	補習教育
28 ☐ latent ability	潜在能力
29 ☐ preside over	司会をする
30 ☐ documentary elimination	書類選考

UNIT 11 Technology / Office Supplies

▶ Key Vocabulary 2-64

この章に出てくる下の英単語の中から日本語訳に当てはまる記号を（　）に記入しましょう。
答え合わせをしたら音声を聞いて英単語を声に出して読み、つづりを書き込み覚えましょう。

●テクノロジー / オフィス用品のトピックに出てくる単語

1. 処理する	（　　）	9. 慣れさせる	（　　）
2. 指揮をする	（　　）	10. 内線	（　　）
3. ホッチキス	（　　）	11. 有益な	（　　）
4. 占有されていない	（　　）	12. 中古の	（　　）
5. 修理する	（　　）	13. 処分する	（　　）
6. 環境保護論者	（　　）	14. 壊れやすい	（　　）
7. 棚卸し	（　　）	15. 一致	（　　）
8. 導入	（　　）	16. 発送する	（　　）

a. environmentalist　　**b.** informative　　**c.** inventory　　**d.** conduct

e. introduction　　**f.** accordance　　**g.** fragile　　**h.** extension

i. dispose　　**j.** fix　　**k.** stapler　　**l.** dispatch

m. process　　**n.** familiarize　　**o.** secondhand　　**p.** unoccupied

LISTENING SECTION

Strategy for Part 1 ≪写真描写問題の解き方≫

「現在進行形の受動態」と「現在完了形の受動態」

下の Warming-Up の写真を見て受動態の形を意識しましょう。

●現在進行形の受動態は「be+ 〜ing+ 過去分詞」で「〜されているところ」という状況を表します。写真に人物が写っていない場合は何かが「誰かに〜されている」という状況である可能性は低いため、間違いの選択肢としても多く出題されます。現在完了形の受動態は「has/have+been+ 過去分詞」で動作が完了した状態を表します。

 Warming-Up 2-65

音声を聞いて（　　）内の語を穴埋めし、
正しい答えはどれか選びましょう。

(A) A (　　　　　　　) has been wrapped by the man.

(B) A man is calculating the (　　　　　　　).

(C) A (　　　　　　　) is being made by card.

(D) A woman is waiting for the (　　　) to be refilled.

正しい答え　(A) (B) (C) (D)

▶ Part 1 Photographs

英文を聞き、 4つの中から最も適切な描写を選びましょう。

Q1.

Ⓐ Ⓑ Ⓒ Ⓓ

Q2.

Ⓐ Ⓑ Ⓒ Ⓓ

Strategy for Part 2 ≪応答問題の解き方≫

否定疑問文など① 否定疑問文（Don't ～? Isn't ～?などで始まる疑問文）

　Part 2 において疑問文が否定で始まったら「～じゃないの？」という意味がすぐに思い浮かぶようにしておきましょう。否定疑問文には多少の不満や、相手を責める気持ちが含まれている場合もあります。答え方は、例えば、Didn't you say ～?「～言わなかったの？」に対して、「言った」なら Yes, (I did.)、「言わなかった」なら No, (I didn't.)、で答えます。

🔵 Warming-Up 🎵2-68

音声を聞いて、疑問文とその正解パターンの答えの意味を記入しましょう。

Q: Didn't you eat your lunch today?

(　　　　　　　　　　　　　　　　　　　　　　　　　　　　　　　)

A: I'll go to the bakery later.　　　◎正解（　　　　　　　　　　　　　）

A: No, I'm too busy.　　　◎正解（　　　　　　　　　　　　　）

A: Oh, I totally forgot about it.　　　◎正解（　　　　　　　　　　　　　）

▶ Part 2 Question-Response

設問に対する応答として、最も適切なものを選びましょう。

Q3. Mark your answer on your answer sheet.　　　Ⓐ Ⓑ Ⓒ

Q4. Mark your answer on your answer sheet.　　　Ⓐ Ⓑ Ⓒ

Q5. Mark your answer on your answer sheet.　　　Ⓐ Ⓑ Ⓒ

Q6. Mark your answer on your answer sheet.　　　Ⓐ Ⓑ Ⓒ

Strategy for Part 3 《会話問題の解き方》

2人の会話問題⑤ Who を含む設問

Part 3 で Who で始まる設問が出てきたら、**話し手のどちらかが何者であるかについて、主に職業を問う設問であることが多いです。**Who is the man?「男性は誰ですか」Who is the woman probably talking to ?「女性はおそらく誰と話していますか」などの形をとります。また、出題される割合は低いですが、話し手以外の会話に出てくる人物について聞かれる場合もあります。

Warming-Up

次の設問を読んで、日本語に訳してから、会話の内容を予測しましょう。

Who most likely are the speakers?

(   )

→会話に出てくる2人は同じ(   ) だと考えられる。

Part 3 Short Conversation

 2-73,74

会話文を聞いて、各設問に対する最も適切な答えを4つの選択肢から選びましょう。

Q7. What are the speakers mainly discussing?

(A) A health check

(B) A broken window

(C) Computer trouble

(D) An aging society

Q8. What does the man suggest the woman do?

(A) Clean up the floor

(B) Order a new computer

(C) Visit her boss

(D) Turn on the power again

Q9. Who does the man say will come later today?

(A) The head of the department

(B) The CEO of the company

(C) One of the IT personnel

(D) An environmentalist

「概要」と「詳細」①

　TOEIC L&R 公開テストの結果が出ると、受験者は「OFFICIAL SCORE CERTIFICATE（公式スコア証明書）」を受け取ります。その最下段には、「**ABILITIES MEASURED**」という、10本の棒グラフが表示されています。

　実はここにTOEIC L&R で求められる能力が示されているのです。例えば、「Part 4 の設問は、**トークの『概要』を問う問題と、『詳細』を問う問題の2つに大別できる**」ということがわかります。つまりPart 4 には、「トークが大まかに聞けているか」と、「トークの詳細情報が聞けているか」という2種類の問題があるのです。まずは比較的正解しやすい『概要』問題から練習してみてはいかがでしょうか。

▶ Warming-Up 🎧 2-75

以下のような、Part 4 の「概要を問う問題」が尋ねていることは何でしょうか。正しいものをそれぞれ1つずつ選び、○で囲みましょう。

① "What is the speaker mainly discussing?" トークの（話題（トピック）・場所）

② "Who most likely is the speaker?" 話し手の（氏名・職業）

▶ Part 4 Short Talk

 2-76,77

説明文を聞いて、各設問に対する最も適切な答えを4つの選択肢から選びましょう。

[List of Extension Numbers]

Extension	Name
212	Ben Jonathan
214	Imtiaz Khan
221	Jun-woo Park
241	Taro Nishiyama

Q10. What is the speaker mainly discussing?

(A) A computer problem　　　　　(B) A software company

(C) An online system　　　　　　(D) An Internet connection

Q11. What does the speaker recommend?

(A) Attending a workshop　　　　(B) Contacting a supervisor

(C) Searching for a solution　　　(D) Downloading an application

Q12. Look at the graphic. Who is the speaker?

(A) Ben Jonathan　　　　　　　　(B) Imtiaz Khan

(C) Jun-woo Park　　　　　　　　(D) Taro Nishiyama

READING SECTION

Strategy for Part 5　≪短文穴埋め問題のための Grammar ≫

文法問題④　「比較級」と「最上級」

　比較級、最上級の問題では、「…と同じくらい～だ」「…より～だ」といった、単純な
ものだけでなく、最上級を使ったさまざまな表現も出題されます。

比較級 **2つのものを比べて「もっと～、より～」という意味**を表します。

最上級 **3つ以上のものを比べて「最も～」の意味**を表します。

☆「比較級」の問題でよく出題されるパターン

①比較級 +than

　（文中に **than** があり、空所に比較級を選ぶパターンで頻出）

　1音節の短い形容詞には形容詞の後に -er をつけて比較級の表現とします。

　My father is taller than my brother.（父は私の兄より背が高いです。）

② more+〈形容詞の原級 / 副詞の原級〉+than

　（〈**more+ 原級**〉を選択肢から選ぶパターンで出現）

　主に比較級となる形容詞、副詞の綴りが長い場合（2音節以上）に more をつけます。

　That bag is more expensive than this one.（あのかばんはこちらのよりも高価です。）

③ the+ 比較級 +S+V,the+ 比較級 +S+V

　（比較級の部分が空所になっていることが多い）

　「…すればするほどますます～」の意味です。

　The older we get, the more intelligent we become.

　（年を取れば取るほど、我々はより賢くなります。）

☆「最上級」の表現のおさらい

① the+〈形容詞 + － est/ 副詞 + － est〉

　Peter is the tallest in his family.（ピーターは家族の中で一番背が高いです。）

② the+〈most+ 形容詞の原級 /most+ 副詞の原級〉

　That ring is the most expensive item in the shop.

　（あの指輪はその店で最も高価な商品です。）

③ one of the+〈最上級 + 名詞の複数形〉

　This is one of the longest holidays I've ever had.

　（この休暇は私が今まででとった最も長い休暇の一つです。）

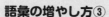

Warming-Up

次に注意すべき比較級と最上級が並んでいます。空欄に当てはまる語を記入しましょう。

good「良い」– better – the best   bad「悪い」–（   ）– the worst

well「元気な」– better – the best

※副詞 well の最上級は best で the はつきませんが、形容詞の場合は the をつけます。

little「少量の、少ない」–（   ）– the least

※比較級の lesser は「価値、重要度がより低い、取るに足りない」の意味で使用します。

late「（時間が）遅い、遅く」– later – the latest

▶ Part 5 Incomplete Sentences

空所に入る最も適切な語句を選びましょう。

Q13. Please send us the color paper we ordered as quickly （   ）.

(A) as you can   (B) possible   (C) than anyone   (D) as often

Q14. Software development proceeded （   ）slower than we had expected.

(A) the better   (B) the more   (C) all   (D) much

Q15. The new vacuum cleaner is （   ）than our competitor's new release.

(A) more efficient   (B) more efficiently   (C) as efficient   (D) efficient

Q16. Mr. Powell is （   ）technician that I've ever seen.

(A) as good as   (B) better   (C) the best   (D) the most

Strategy for Part 6 ≪長文穴埋め問題の解き方≫

語彙の増やし方③

　Unit 6 で紹介した Part 6 の設問「1. 文脈に関係なく解ける問題」のうち、「品詞を選ぶ問題（通称・品詞問題）」について説明します。

　TOEIC L&R の Part 6 全 16 問中、ほぼ毎回出題される「品詞問題」は、あまり前後の文脈を考える必要がなく、**空欄の前後を見るだけで解答できる場合がほとんどです。**よって、このタイプの問題を解く際も、例えば動詞を覚える際は「動詞＋目的語」、形容詞を覚える際は「形容詞＋名詞」というように、TOEIC L&R に頻繁に出てくる単語同士を組み合わせ、フレーズ（語句のかたまり）で覚える習慣が大きく役立ちます。

　また、英語の品詞は大半が「接尾辞（語尾）」で区別できます。**名詞、動詞、形容詞、副詞の 4 つについては、よく見かける語尾を今すぐに覚えましょう。**

▶ Part 6 Text Completion

次の英文を読んで、選択肢の中から空所に入る最も適切な語句を選びましょう。

From: Elly Baker, General Affairs Section
To: All new employees
Subject: Seminar series
Date: May 11

Dear new colleagues,

I am writing to let you know that our company offers all new employees a series of lectures on computers for free every year. ------ advanced computer skills are **17.** needed in our industry, your attendance is highly recommended. Since all the seminars are provided by experienced instructors from some of the leading computer schools in the area, they will be ------ and helpful with your everyday **18** work. ------ . Thus, your applications will be processed on a first-come-first- **19.** served basis. The date and venue ------ today. For further information, please **20.** contact us at extension 210 or Mr. Hogan at extension 252.

Best regards,
Elly

Q17. (A) Despite of
(C) In addition to
(B) Considering that
(D) On the contrary

Q18. (A) informed
(C) inform
(B) informative
(D) information

Q19. (A) We have sufficient number of computers for you all.
(B) I know you will be allocated to your sections next week.
(C) I understand that you are too busy to attend.
(D) The number of seats is limited to 50.

Q20. (A) will be announced
(C) will be announcing
(B) will announce
(D) will have announced

「繰り返し解くこと」の意味

　　TOEIC L&R 対策で、「正解も覚えてしまったのに、同じ問題を何度も解くことに意味はありますか？」という質問を受けることがあります。「解き直す**方法によっては、大きな効果**が期待できます」と答えています。

　　Part 7 を解く際に、皆さんが欲しいスキルは何でしょう。多くの人は「速く的確に文脈（ストーリー）を読み取る力」を望んでいるのではないでしょうか。では、この「速読力（1 分間で約 200 語を読むイメージ）」をつけるにはどうしたらよいのでしょう。

　　一例ですが、①文書内の語彙・文法を全てチェック、②文書の内容を完全に理解、③その文書を暗記するくらい繰り返し音読、することが有効です。Part 7 に出てくる文書はたいてい日常生活に関係したもので、同じような内容の文書がよく見受けられます。①～③を実践するうちに、「**TOEIC 的なストーリー**」に**慣れる**こともできるのです。

▶ Part 7 Single Passage

次の英文を読んで、設問に対する答えとして最も適切なものを選択肢の中から選びましょう。

 http://www.xxxx/xxxx/

Procedure for Recycling Your PC

Do you have an old PC in storage that you don't use anymore? Evergreen PC, Ltd. can help you sell it at the highest price or dispose of it in an eco-friendly way. Please see the instructions below:

1. Check if your PC is still working

We can come to your home or office to check its condition. If your PC is working fine, we will evaluate it and give you our approximate secondhand purchase price immediately. Even if your PC is not working properly, you can dispose of it free of charge. You don't have to decide if you sell or dispose of it at this time.

Note: Although it depends on the town where you live in, disposing of just one PC will normally cost you 10 pounds on average.

2. Complete the form

Whether you sell or dispose of your PC, you will need to complete a form of acceptance. The form can be downloaded from this Web site.

3. Send your PC to us

Please send us your PC as a fragile item along with the correct form at the following address by express mail. We will cover the shipping costs.

Evergreen PC, Ltd.   12 Gower Street, Ashley, Aberdeen AB10 5PZ

Once we've received your PC and checked its condition more precisely, we will inform you of our final evaluation by e-mail. Then please let us know your final decision if you want us to sell it, dispose of it or send it back to you within two business days.

4. When we dispose of your PC

If your PC is too hard to repair, it will be taken apart and any parts in good condition will be sent to recycling companies. Also, we are an industrial waste disposal operator certified by the city. Your PC will be disposed of in a safe way in accordance with city regulations.

Q21. Who is the instruction most likely intended for?

(A) Parts suppliers

(B) Appliance stores

(C) Internet providers

(D) Computer users

Q22. What does Evergreen PC, Ltd. do for its customers?

(A) Fills out forms

(B) Dispatches components

(C) Picks up their computers

(D) Evaluates their items

Q23. What is available on the Web site?

(A) An estimate

(B) An acceptance form

(C) A list of parts

(D) A voucher

Q24. The word "certified" in paragraph 5, line 4, is closest in meaning to

(A) authorized

(B) criticized

(C) identified

(D) equalized

Q25. What is suggested about the procedure?

(A) Customers have to pay a deposit.

(B) A document needs to be submitted online.

(C) The company comes to pick up used machines.

(D) Items beyond repair cannot be sold.

▶ ボキャブラリーアルファ 11 Technology / Office Supplies

この章のトピックでよく出る単語と表現です。日本語訳を見ながら英単語を声に出して言ってみましょう。

●テクノロジー / オフィス用品のトピックに出てくる単語 2-78

1 ☐	**routine**	[ru:tí:n]	名	日常業務
2 ☐	**paperwork**	[péipəwə́:k]	名	書類仕事
3 ☐	**disseminate**	[disémənèit]	動	広める
4 ☐	**cubicle**	[kjú:bikl]	名	仕事スペース
5 ☐	**briefcase**	[brí:fkèis]	名	書類カバン
6 ☐	**license**	[láis(ə)ns]	名	免許、認可
7 ☐	**scrutiny**	[skrú:t(ə)ni]	名	精密調査
8 ☐	**calculation**	[kælkjəléiʃən]	名	計算
9 ☐	**prospective**	[prəspéktiv]	形	将来の、予想される
10 ☐	**defect**	[dí:fekt]	名	欠陥
11 ☐	**discrepancy**	[diskrép(ə)nsi]	名	不一致
12 ☐	**confusion**	[kənfjú:ʒən]	名	混乱
13 ☐	**letterhead**	[létəhéd]	名	レターヘッド
14 ☐	**duration**	[d(j)u(ə)réiʃən]	名	存続、期間
15 ☐	**perspective**	[pə(r)spéktiv]	名	見通し
16 ☐	**adjustment**	[ədʒʌ́stmənt]	名	調整
17 ☐	**cupboard**	[kʌ́bə(r)]	名	棚
18 ☐	**influence**	[ínfluəns]	動	影響する
19 ☐	**release**	[rilí:s]	動	解放する
20 ☐	**remote**	[rimóut]	形	遠い、離れた

●テクノロジー / オフィス用品のトピックに出てくる表現 2-79

21 ☐	**go ahead**	前に進む、許可する
22 ☐	**technical jargon**	専門用語
23 ☐	**peripheral equipment**	周辺装置
24 ☐	**fluorescent light**	蛍光灯
25 ☐	**bulletin board**	掲示板
26 ☐	**head office**	本社
27 ☐	**security guard**	警備員
28 ☐	**image processing**	画像処理
29 ☐	**trade show**	展示会、商品見本市
30 ☐	**automatic bank transfer**	銀行自動振り込み

▶ Key Vocabulary

🎧 2-80

この章に出てくる下の英単語の中から日本語訳に当てはまる記号を（　）に記入しましょう。答え合わせをしたら音声を聞いて英単語を声に出して読み、つづりを書き込み覚えましょう。

● 交通のトピックに出てくる単語

1.	神社	（　）	9.	渋滞	（　）
2.	氾濫させる	（　）	10.	迂回路	（　）
3.	利用できる	（　）	11.	評判	（　）
4.	歩行者	（　）	12.	不便	（　）
5.	歩道橋	（　）	13.	交通	（　）
6.	特徴	（　）	14.	坂	（　）
7.	通勤する	（　）	15.	正確に	（　）
8.	表示板	（　）	16.	身分証明	（　）

a. shrine **b.** detour **c.** flood **d.** precisely

e. identification **f.** pedestrian **g.** feature **h.** accessible

i. signboard **j.** slope **k.** inconvenience **l.** traffic

m. commute **n.** congestion **o.** reputation **p.** overpass

LISTENING SECTION

Strategy for Part 1 ≪写真描写問題の解き方≫

似ている音の聞き取り②

下の Warming-Up の写真に出てくるものと似ている音を探しましょう。

● Unit 7 と同様、写真の中に出てくるものと発音の似ている音が選択肢に出てくる場合にこれが正解であるかどうか識別する必要があります。ちなみに「路面電車」のことは trolley, street car などで表現します。

 Warming-Up 🎧 2-81

音声を聞いて（　　　）内の語を穴埋めし、
正しい答えはどれか選びましょう。

(A) A (　　　　　　) is running through the city.
(B) The (　　　　) is occupied by people.
(C) (　　　　　　) are displayed outdoors.
(D) People are riding (　　　　) bikes to get around.

正しい答え　(A) (B) (C) (D)

113

▶ Part 1 Photographs

英文を聞き、4つの中から最も適切な描写を選びましょう。

Q1.

Ⓐ Ⓑ Ⓒ Ⓓ

Q2.

Ⓐ Ⓑ Ⓒ Ⓓ

Strategy for Part 2 ≪応答問題の解き方≫

否定疑問文など② 選択疑問文（AかBか選ぶ疑問文）

　設問中に A or B という、「A か B か」の表現が入る選択疑問文に対しての答え方は「Aのみ」、「Bのみ」、「どちらでもよい」、「どちらも不可」、「未定」などのパターンがあります。

 Warming-Up　🎵 2-84

音声を聞いて、疑問文とその正解パターンの答えの意味を記入しましょう。

Q: Are you going to take the bus or the train? (　　　　　　　　)

A: I'll take the subway.　　　　　◎正解 (　　　　　　　　)

A: Neither, I came here by car.　　◎正解 (　　　　　　　　)

A: Let me check the timetable first. ◎正解 (　　　　　　　　)

▶ Part 2 Question-Response

設問に対する応答として、最も適切なものを選びましょう。

Q3. Mark your answer on your answer sheet.　　Ⓐ Ⓑ Ⓒ

Q4. Mark your answer on your answer sheet.　　Ⓐ Ⓑ Ⓒ

Q5. Mark your answer on your answer sheet.　　Ⓐ Ⓑ Ⓒ

Q6. Mark your answer on your answer sheet.　　Ⓐ Ⓑ Ⓒ

Strategy for Part 3 《会話問題の解き方》

2人の会話問題⑥　**How** を含む設問

　Part 3 の設問のうち How で始まる疑問文は How did he arrive at the airport?
「彼はどうやって空港に到着しましたか」のように手段や方法を問う問題の場合と、
How much「いくら」、How soon「どれくらい早く」、How long「どれくらい長く」
など、具体的な数値を問う場合があります。

🔵 Warming-Up

次の設問を読んで、日本語に訳してから、会話の内容を予測しましょう。

　How long has the woman worked for the company?

　(　　　　　　　　　　　　　　　　　　　　　　　　　　　　　　)

→女性が一定の期間 (　　　　　　　　　　) と考えられる。

▶ Part 3　Short Conversation

 2-89,90

会話文を聞いて、各設問に対する最も適切な答えを4つの選択肢から選びましょう。

Q7. Where does the conversation probably take place?

(A) At a bus terminal　　　(B) At a train station

(C) At a parking lot　　　(D) At an airport

Q8. What does the woman say about herself?

(A) She did not see the signboard.

(B) She lives in Oxford.

(C) She works only on weekdays.

(D) She is new to this town.

Q9. How many times does the train to Oxford leave this station per hour at the
weekend?

(A) 3 times　　　(B) 4 times

(C) 6 times　　　(D) 8 times

「図表問題」の解き方②

　「図表問題（グラフや図などを見ながら解く問題）」で出題される図表の中に、「地図系」のものがあります。多いのは「フロア・マップ」や「ルート・マップ」です。また、選択肢はたいてい (A) Room 1, (B) Room 2, … のようになっています。このような図表は、どこに注意すべきでしょうか。

　当然ながら、トークの中で「Room 1」などと言うことはないでしょう。それでは図表が不要になってしまいます。しかし、よく図を見ると、「Supply Room（備品室）」などが載っていたりします。このような「目印になる場所」はトーク内で必ず言及されます。それがヒントになる語句ですので、注意して聴いてみてください。

🍐 Warming-Up

以下のような、場所を表すヒントが示していることは何でしょうか。それぞれ正しいものをそれぞれ1つずつ選び、○で囲みましょう。

① "next to the reception"（入口・受付）の（となり・手前）
② "between the vending machine and the photocopier"（自販機・両替機）と（写真屋・コピー機）の間

▶ Part 4 Short Talk

 2-91,92

説明文を聞いて、各設問に対する最も適切な答えを4つの選択肢から選びましょう。

Q10. What is the broadcast mainly about?

(A) The event schedule　　(B) A traffic update

(C) Road repair　　(D) Ticket information

Q11. Look at the graphic. On which route will

the shuttle operate?

(A) Road A

(B) Road B

(C) Road C

(D) Road D

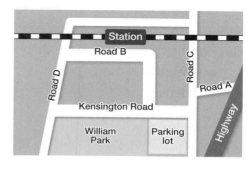

Q12. What are the listeners advised to do until 10 p.m.?

(A) Use public transportation

(B) Stay at the venue

(C) Pay attention to announcements

(D) Keep their parking tickets

READING SECTION

Strategy for Part 5 ≪短文穴埋め問題のための Grammar ≫

文法問題⑤ 「仮定法」と「倒置」のケース

　　If, would, unless, should などを選択肢に含む問題が出題されたら、**仮定法を問われている可能性**があります。

☆**「仮定法」には公式がある**

「もし…なら」の意味の文を「条件文」と言います。条件文の中で「もし、私が鳥だったらいいのに」のように、**事実に反する仮定**（「私」はという主語の人物は決して鳥になれませんから、事実に反します）を表すことがあります。**この時の動詞の形を「仮定法」**と言います。難しく聞こえますが、仮定法には決まった公式がありますので、あてはめて考えましょう。

●**仮定法の公式**

	if 節の中の動詞の形	帰結節の中の動詞の形
現在の事実に反する仮定 （＝仮定法過去）	過去形 If I <u>were</u> you,	助動詞の過去形 (would,could,might)＋ 動詞の原形 I would <u>accept</u> the request.
過去の事実に反する仮定 （＝仮定法過去完了）	過去完了形 If I <u>had had</u> enough money,	助動詞の過去形 (would,could,might)＋ 〈have+ 過去分詞〉 I could have <u>bought</u> the watch.

①**基本形** 　**if 節**「もし〜なら」「…だったなら」

　　　　　　＋**帰結節**「〜なのに」「〜だったのに」

②**if 節に should を使う条件文**もあります。

　　If he should fail, he would ask for my advice.

　　（もし彼が失敗したら彼は私のアドバイスを求めるでしょう。）

☆**「倒置」の起こる場合と、その語順**

「倒置」とは、S＋V が語句の強調のために V＋S（もしくは助動詞＋S）の語順になることです。倒置の起こるケースについて学習しましょう。

①**否定語が文頭に来る場合**

　　<u>Not only</u> **is he** kind, <u>but</u> he is <u>also</u> competent.（彼は親切なだけでなく、有能です。）

②**if が省略**された場合

　　Should he fail, he would ask for my advice.

　　（もし彼が失敗したら、私にアドバイスを求めるでしょう。）

③**so, neither ,nor で文や節が始まる場合**

　　(A) I cannot swim.（私は泳げません。）

　　(B) **Neither can I**.（私もです。）

Warming-Up

次は「…がなければ」、「…がなかったら」の意味を表す表現に関する表です。空欄に当てはまる語を記入しましょう。

	条件節（もしくは前置詞句）		主節
仮定法過去 「（今）…がなければ」	・If it were not for ・(　　　　) it not for ・If not for ・But for ・Without	＋名詞	主語 + 助動詞の過去形 (would, could, might)+ 動詞の原形
仮定法過去完了 （あの時） 「…がなかったら」	・If it (　　　　) been for ・Had it not been for ・If not for ・But for ・Without	＋名詞	主語 + 助動詞の過去形 (would, could, might)+ 〈have+ 過去分詞〉

▶ Part 5 Incomplete Sentences

空所に入る最も適切な語句を選びましょう。

Q13. If I (　　　) in your position, I would ask to speak with the director.

    (A) were   (B) was   (C) had   (D) am

Q14. I think it (　　) easy to get the job.

    (A) did   (B) would be   (C) being   (D) will

Q15. If it (　　) not been for your help, I would have failed.

    (A) will   (B) were   (C) had   (D) have

Q16. Under no circumstances must the president's office (　　) left unlocked.

    (A) be   (B) should   (C) is   (D) will be

Strategy for Part 6 ≪長文穴埋め問題の解き方≫

語彙の増やし方④

　Unit 7 で紹介した Part 6 の設問「2. 文脈に沿って解く問題」のうち、「**文と文をつなぐ語句（接続副詞・つなぎ言葉）を選ぶ問題**」について説明します。

　TOEIC L&R の Part 6 全 16 問中、2, 3 問程度出題されるこのタイプの問題に解答するには、空欄を含む文の前後の文脈を考えなければならず、一見大変そうかもしれません。

　しかし、よく出る「つなぎ言葉」は、実はそれほど多くありません（Therefore, However, Meanwhile, Besides, Consequently など 10 個程度）。**接続詞、前置詞（を含むもの）と併せて一気に覚えておく**ことをお勧めします。ちなみに、皆さんが英文を書く際、and や but ばかり使わずにこの「つなぎ言葉」を使うと、英文がよりフォーマルになります。TOEIC L&R（Listening & Speaking）、**実は Writing に活かすこともできる**のです。

▶ Part 6 Text Completion

次の英文を読んで、選択肢の中から空所に入る最も適切な語句を選びましょう。

Tomorrow's Train Service Suspended on the Northern Line

To all passengers:

Due to construction work between Kentish Station and Acton Station, the Northern Line will be out of ------- from 11:00 A.M. to 2:00 P.M. tomorrow.
17.
Passengers bound for Central Park ------- to take a detour; for example, take the
18.
Green Line and change to the Blue Line at the next station. During the construction work, we will also operate a temporary bus service to Acton Station from the bus terminal near the West Exit ------- you can easily get to your
19.
destination. -------. We apologize for any inconvenience this may cause you.
20.

Q17. (A) order　　　(B) stock　　　(C) time　　　(D) service

Q18. (A) will advise　　(B) are advised　　(C) will be advising　　(D) have advised

Q19. (A) such as　　(B) now that　　(C) so as to　　(D) so that

Q20. (A) We look forward to travelling with you soon.
　　　(B) The train service will resume the day after tomorrow.
　　　(C) For further information, please feel free to ask the station staff.
　　　(D) The new station building will be opened next month.

Strategy for Part 7 ≪読解問題の解き方≫

音声によるリーディング練習

　最近、Part 7 を扱っている「公式 TOEIC L&R 問題集」や一部の TOEIC L&R 対策本には英語ネイティヴ・スピーカーが文書を音読した音声ファイルなどが付属されるようになっています。「リーディングなのに音声」、いったいこれはなぜでしょう。

　Unit 11 でも述べた通り、Part 7 では一定の読解スピードが求められます。速読の練習法の一つとして、**「音声のスピードに合わせて、目で英文を追う」**という方法が一般的になりつつあるのです。これを続けると、**「英文を左から右に読む（右から左に戻らない）」**習慣が身につきます。結果的に、**読むスピードも上がる**のです。考えてみれば、**英語とは本来、「左から右に」読み書きする言語**ですよね。次の Part 7 を活用して、音声によるリーディング練習をしてみましょう。

▶ Part 7 Double Passages

 2-93,94

次の英文を読んで、設問に対する答えとして最も適切なものを選択肢の中から選びましょう。

◀ ▶ http://www.xxxx/xxxx/ ▼

What you can do with the updated ticket machines

For greater convenience, Plymouth Trains updated its ticket machines at some stations on May 11. Now they allow customers to purchase tickets far more easily, and they also show seat availability more precisely than before. Please see the following features of our new system:

1. New Payment Method

Payments can now be made by smartphone as well as cash and credit card now that the machines have been installed at the stations. After you input your destination and the number of tickets required, fares will show up on the screen. Then, customers can make their payment by inserting their card or cash or by placing their smart phone in front of the reader on the machine. For smartphone payments, you need to have the "Fast Pay" app installed on your smartphone beforehand.

2. Seating Charts

With the updated ticket machine, customers can book the seats exactly where they prefer to sit. By touching the "seating arrangement" button, the seating map of the train will appear on the screen. Then, please select the seats you prefer.

3. Order in Advance

Please note that customers can make reservations for the seats up to one month before boarding. Also, this new seat reservation system will be available on your computer devices from August.

We look forward to travelling with you soon.

Customer Support Team, Plymouth Trains Co., Ltd.

```
●●●                          E-mail

Dear Customer Support Team,

Hello. I tried to book two seats on the train to New Ark for July 24 on my
laptop, but the seating map didn't show up on the screen. Therefore, I cannot
proceed to the stage of payment with my PC. Do I have to go to the nearest
station to buy the tickets, or is there anything I can do from home?

Cary Meyer
```

Q21. What is the purpose of the Web page?

    (A) To promote a special sale

    (B) To invite customers to an event

    (C) To announce the latest changes

    (D) To report a technical problem

Q22. What are customers asked to do before they pay with a smartphone?

    (A) Check their bank account

    (B) Download an application

    (C) Bring their photo identification

    (D) Update their personal information

Q23. From when can Mr. Meyer reserve his seats?

    (A) May 11   (B) June 11

    (C) June 24   (D) July 24

Q24. What will the Customer Support Team probably advise Mr. Meyer to do?

    (A) Enter the promotional code

    (B) Pay with his credit card

    (C) Contact a PC repair shop

    (D) Purchase at the station

Q25. What is NOT mentioned about the machines?

    (A) They have been recently renewed.

    (B) They are installed at all stations.

    (C) They show customers more seating details.

    (D) They provide customers with more payment options.

▶ ボキャブラリーアルファ 12 Transportation

この章のトピックでよく出る単語と表現です。日本語訳を見ながら英単語を声に出して言ってみましょう。

●交通のトピックに出てくる単語

 2-95

1 ☐	**approach** [əpróutʃ]	動	近づく、接近する	
2 ☐	**irritate** [íritèit]	動	じらす、苛立たせる	
3 ☐	**freight** [fréit]	名	貨物、貨物輸送	
4 ☐	**translation** [trænsléiʃən]	名	翻訳	
5 ☐	**logistics** [lo(u)dʒístiks]	名	物流管理、ロジスティックス	
6 ☐	**offset** [ɔ(:)fsét]	動	相殺する、埋め合わせる	
7 ☐	**fare** [féə(r)]	名	運賃	
8 ☐	**hamper** [hǽmpə(r)]	動	妨げる	
9 ☐	**substantially** [səbstǽnʃəli]	形	実質的に	
10 ☐	**tedious** [tí:diəs]	形	退屈な	
11 ☐	**tier** [tíə(r)]	名	段、層	
12 ☐	**streamline** [strí:mláin]	動	合理化する、簡素化する	
13 ☐	**desire** [dizáiə(r)]	動	望む	
14 ☐	**smooth** [smú:ð]	形	なめらかな、すべすべした	
15 ☐	**directory** [dirékt(ə)ri]	名	住所氏名録	
16 ☐	**carton** [ká:(r)tn]	名	段ボール箱、収納箱	
17 ☐	**operate** [áp(ə)rèit]	動	運営する	
18 ☐	**depot** [dí:pou]	名	倉庫	
19 ☐	**successive** [səksésiv]	形	連続する、継続的な	
20 ☐	**punctually** [pʌ́ŋktʃuəli]	副	時間通りに	

●交通のトピックに出てくる表現

 2-96

21 ☐	**paved road**	舗装道路
22 ☐	**move up**	前進する
23 ☐	**open to**	解放されている、受けやすい
24 ☐	**fare adjustment office**	運賃精算所
25 ☐	**multiple collision**	玉突き衝突
26 ☐	**shipping cost**	運送費
27 ☐	**median strip**	中央分離帯
28 ☐	**toll road**	有料道路
29 ☐	**taxi stand**	タクシー乗り場
30 ☐	**pass permit**	通行証

▶ Key Vocabulary

 3-01

この章に出てくる下の英単語の中から日本語訳に当てはまる記号を（　）に記入しましょう。
答え合わせをしたら音声を聞いて英単語を声に出して読み、つづりを書き込み覚えましょう。

● 旅行 / 空港のトピックに出てくる単語

1. 点検する	（　　）	9. わがまま	（　　）
2. 客船	（　　）	10. 代わりの	（　　）
3. 飲み物	（　　）	11. 回答	（　　）
4. 廊下	（　　）	12. 通勤客	（　　）
5. 管理者	（　　）	13. 減少する	（　　）
6. 出発	（　　）	14. 豊富な	（　　）
7. 故障	（　　）	15. 穀物	（　　）
8. 購入する	（　　）	16. 忠実な	（　　）

a. breakdown **b.** purchase **c.** reply **d.** corridor

e. administrator **f.** grain **g.** alternative **h.** faithful

i. selfish **j.** inspect **k.** departure **l.** liner

m. abundant **n.** beverage **o.** commuter **p.** decrease

LISTENING SECTION

Strategy for Part 1 ≪写真描写問題の解き方≫

複数の人物に共通すること

下の Warming-Up の写真を見ながら複数の人物に共通する動作の表現を確認しましょう。

● 複数の人物が写真に写っていて、一人の人物が目立っていない場合には、人物に共通する動作や、周りのものを表した表現が正解になることがあります。動詞だけでなく、主語が正しく複数人物を表しているかについても確認しましょう

● **Warming-Up** 3-02

音声を聞いて（　　　）内の語を穴埋めし、
正しい答えはどれか選びましょう。

(A) Performers are (　　　　　　) inside the palace.

(B) People are (　　　　　) along the street.

(C) People are (　　　　　　) in the same direction.

(D) People in uniforms are (　　　　　) with firearms.　　正しい答え　(A) (B) (C) (D)

▶ Part 1 Photographs

英文を聞き、4つの中から最も適切な描写を選びましょう。

Q1.

Ⓐ Ⓑ Ⓒ Ⓓ

Q2.

Ⓐ Ⓑ Ⓒ Ⓓ

....

Strategy for Part 2 ≪応答問題の解き方≫

否定疑問文など③　付加疑問文（〜ですよね、と確認する疑問文）

　設問の最後が〜 don't you?、〜 is it?、〜 isn't it? などで終わり、「ですよね？」、「ではないですよね？」と確認するのが付加疑問文です。答え方は否定疑問文の時と同じで、肯定するなら Yes, しないなら No, で答えましょう。

🔵 Warming-Up 🎧 3-05

音声を聞いて、疑問文とその正解パターンの答えの意味を記入しましょう。

Q: The new itinerary is ready, isn't it?　（　　　　　　　　　　）
A: Lisa is going to distribute it.　◎正解（　　　　　　　　　）
A: It'll be ready by tomorrow.　◎正解（　　　　　　　　　）
A: No, not yet.　◎正解（　　　　　　　　　）

▶ Part 2 Question-Response

 3-06,07,08,09

設問に対する応答として、最も適切なものを選びましょう。

Q3. Mark your answer on your answer sheet.　Ⓐ Ⓑ Ⓒ
Q4. Mark your answer on your answer sheet.　Ⓐ Ⓑ Ⓒ
Q5. Mark your answer on your answer sheet.　Ⓐ Ⓑ Ⓒ
Q6. Mark your answer on your answer sheet.　Ⓐ Ⓑ Ⓒ

Strategy for Part 3　≪会話問題の解き方≫

図表を含む問題③　Why を含む設問

　Part 3 の設問のうち Why で始まる設問は「理由」「原因」を聞いています。Why did the man call the office?「男性はなぜオフィスに電話しましたか」など、人物の行動の理由を聞いたり、Why was the flight canceled? 「なぜ飛行機はキャンセルになりましたか」など物事の原因を聞いたりする設問があります。会話の前後の状況を理解しながら聞き取る必要があるでしょう。

⏺ Warming-Up

次の設問を読んで、日本語に訳してみましょう。

Why does the customer send an e-mail to the shop?

(　　　　　　　　　　　　　　　　　　　　　　　　　　　　)

▶ Part 3　Short Conversation

 3-10,11

会話文を聞いて、各設問に対する最も適切な答えを 4 つの選択肢から選びましょう。

Gate	Destination	Departure time
S12	San Diego	8:20 A.M.
N18	Orlando	9:30 A.M.
N31	Paris	11:30 A.M.
S25	Seattle	1:10 P.M.

Q7. Why doesn't the man have any suitcases?

(A) He's already checked them in.

(B) He gave them to the administrators.

(C) He didn't bring them.

(D) He decided to leave them in the airport.

Q8. What are the speakers going to do at the event?

(A) Distribute handouts　　　(B) Attend a charity show

(C) Pick up the presenter　　(D) Make a presentation

Q9. Look at the graphic. Which city are the speakers flying to?

(A) San Diego　　　(B) Orlando

(C) Paris　　　(D) Seattle

「概要」と「詳細」②

　Part 4 では、1 つのトークにつき 3 問の設問が出題されますが、通常、『概要』を問う問題は 1 問目に、『詳細』を問う問題は 2、3 問目に来ます（中には『概要』を問う問題が全くない場合もありますが）。では、この 2 種類の設問のヒントが、トークの中ではどのように出てくるのでしょうか。

　一般に、『概要問題』のヒントは、トークのあちらこちらにあります（例：「切符」「運賃」「ホーム」「係員」などの語句が聞こえ、「これは駅でのアナウンスだ」と推測する）。一方『詳細問題』のヒントは、基本的に 1 度しか出てきません。**設問の並び順にこだわらず、1 問目の『概要問題』はいつでも解けると考え、まず 2、3 問目の『詳細問題』に集中してみてもよいかもしれません。**

⏺ Warming-Up 🎧 3-12

以下のような、Part 4 の「概要を問う問題」が尋ねていることは何でしょうか。正しいものをそれぞれ 1 つずつ選び、○で囲みましょう。

① "Where is the announcement taking place?" アナウンスの（内容・場所）
② "What type of business does the speaker work for?" 話し手の（職場・職歴）

▶ Part 4 Short Talk

 3-13,14

説明文を聞いて、各設問に対する最も適切な答えを 4 つの選択肢から選びましょう。

Q10. Where is the announcement probably being made?

(A) On a bus

(B) On a train

(C) At a station

(D) At an airport

Q11. What is the cause of the problem?

(A) Some passengers cannot get a refund.

(B) Some roads are under repair.

(C) There is no alternative transportation.

(D) There has been a technical problem.

Q12. What are the listeners in a hurry advised to do?

(A) Show a certificate

(B) Speak to the staff

(C) Go to the office

(D) Take the subway

READING SECTION

Strategy for Part 5 ≪短文穴埋め問題のための Grammar ≫

語彙問題① 「不定詞」と「動名詞」の使い分け

　語彙の問題は多岐にわたり、それぞれの用法を丁寧に覚えるのが英語力向上のための確実な方法です。しかし、そのうち多くの問題に使用できる戦略は Unit 4 で説明した「**自動詞と他動詞の使い分け**」の他に、①**不定詞と動名詞の使い分け**、②**動詞の後に続く前置詞との相性の見極め**（Unit 14 で説明します）、などがあります。ここでは①について説明します。

☆不定詞と動名詞を使い分ける問題

　不定詞を目的語にとる語と、動名詞を目的語にとる語のどちらかを選ぶ場合には空所の後に何が続くかをみましょう。

「**to 不定詞**」だけを目的語にとる動詞には

　want, hope, promise, agree, decide, mean, offer, wish など、

　「〜したい」「〜するつもりだ」の意味の動詞が多いです。

「**動名詞**」だけを目的語にとる動詞には

　enjoy, avoid, deny, mind, stop, consider, finish など、

　「〜し終える」「熟考する」「避ける」の意味が多いです。

「**to 不定詞**」も「**動名詞**」も目的語にとる動詞には

remember	remember to 不定詞	（忘れないで…する）
	remember 〜 ing	（…したことを覚えている）
forget	forget to 不定詞	（…するのを忘れる）
	forget 〜 ing	（…したことを忘れる）などがあります。

● Warming-Up

動名詞を使った慣用表現の文の日本語訳を書きましょう。

(1) Dr. Horton is accustomed to taking care of selfish patients.

　（　　　　　　　　　　　　　　　　　　　　　　　　　）

(2) Upon arriving at the hotel, you must check your luggage.

　（　　　　　　　　　　　　　　　　　　　　　　　　　）

(3) I'm looking forward to seeing you in the next summer vacation.

　（　　　　　　　　　　　　　　　　　　　　　　　　　）

▶ Part 5 Incomplete Sentences

空所に入る最も適切な語句を選びましょう。

Q13. You should leave now (　　) the rain storm.

    (A) avoid   (B) avoiding

    (C) to avoiding   (D) to avoid

Q14. Have you received any kind of (　　) to our inquiry about the size of the monitor?

    (A) reply   (B) operation

    (C) question   (D) prevention

Q15. The mayor is considering (　　) its tree planting campaign to better serve the companies.

    (A) redesign   (B) to redesign

    (C) redesigning   (D) redesigned

Q16. Upon (　　) of the new station building, the shop will open to meet the commuters' needs.

    (A) complete   (B) completion

    (C) completed   (D) completing

Strategy for Part 6 《長文穴埋め問題の解き方》

文法②

　Unit 7 で紹介した Part 6 の設問「2. 文脈に沿って解く問題」のうち、「**動詞の形を選ぶ問題**」について説明します。

　TOEIC L&R の Part 6 **全 16 問中、2 問程度**出題されるこのタイプの問題ですが、まず文法的には、**①時制、②態の 2 つを理解する必要**があります。その上で、例えば空欄に「過去形」「現在形」「未来表現」のどれが入るかを問われているとします。まず、文法的に誤りとなる選択肢をはずすと、文法的に正しい選択肢が複数残ります。この複数の選択肢からさらに正解を選ぶためには…空欄を含む文の前後の文を読み、時制を決める必要があります。「『文法力・語彙力』を問う Part 5、『読解力』を問う Part 7、そしてこの両者のスキルを問うのが Part 6 である」ととらえると、Part 6 の本質がわかるかもしれません。

▶ Part 6 Text Completion

次の英文を読んで、選択肢の中から空所に入る最も適切な語句を選びましょう。

Summer Walking Tour in the Highlands

Have you decided on your plans for the summer holidays yet? If not, Owens Travel can provide you with some very attractive tour plans. ------ staying at the beach is popular in summer, how about having a great time walking in the beautiful mountains? We would like to recommend walking in the Highlands this summer. Some of you may worry about your ------ hiking experience, but please do not be concerned. Experienced certified tour guides, who are familiar with the area, ------ to you. Having lunch on the top of a beautiful mountain will be an unforgettable experience! Also, the tour includes visits to some other popular tourist attractions, such as historical castles and a beautiful lake. ------ .

Q17. (A) While   (B) Furthermore
     (C) During   (D) Given that

Q18. (A) lack of   (B) a little
     (C) most of   (D) a few

Q19. (A) will be attended   (B) attends
     (C) have attended   (D) will attend

Q20. (A) The number of visitors has been decreasing.
     (B) Please check the itinerary you have received.
     (C) You need to contact the guides during their business hours.
     (D) This tour is very popular every year, so please reserve early.

「英語で考える」とは？

　皆さんは、英語ネイティヴの先生などから、「英語で考えなさい」「頭で日本語を使わずに読みなさい」というようなアドバイスを受けたことはありませんか。そして、「自分はどうしても日本語で考えてしまう…」などと悩んだりしていませんか。

　「英語を英語のまま理解する」はある種の理想であり、「それができれば苦労しない」となります（一方、「英語で考える」ようになると、日本語を読む際に苦労します）。しかし実際は、日本語を母語として日本で育った人の場合、かなり高度な英語力を持ちながらも、「日本語で（も）考えている」人は少なくないのです。

　もちろん、それは全く悪い事ではありません。Part 7 で文書を読む練習をする際、例えば、日本語で考えながらも、「語順」だけ英語と同じように左から右に読むなど、**まずは自分が無理なくできる練習方法を探してみてください。**

▶ Part 7 Triple Passages

次の英文を読んで、設問に対する答えとして最も適切なものを選択肢の中から選びましょう。

Hamley's Bakery

Being blessed with abundant pure water and rich soil, Laurence Village is one of the most famous areas for the production of high-quality wheat in this country. Ever since Sir Thomas Hamley established his bakery in 1851, we have been producing the finest bread, which is well-known as "Hamley's bread", a specialty product of the village. The bakery is open from 9:00 A.M. to 3:00 P.M. on weekdays, but we close earlier if the bread sells out. We also welcome visitors to our factory. Tours take place three times a day. Please note that there is a very limited number of parking spaces for shoppers behind the shop. For further information, please visit our Web site at www.hamleysbakery.com.

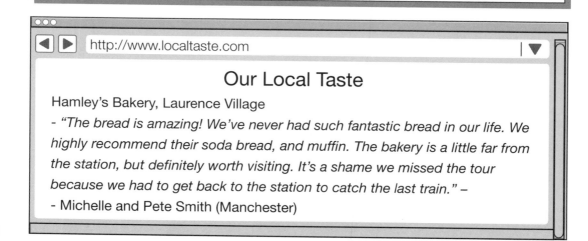

http://www.localtaste.com

Our Local Taste

Hamley's Bakery, Laurence Village

- *"The bread is amazing! We've never had such fantastic bread in our life. We highly recommend their soda bread, and muffin. The bakery is a little far from the station, but definitely worth visiting. It's a shame we missed the tour because we had to get back to the station to catch the last train."* –
- Michelle and Pete Smith (Manchester)

E-mail

Dear Mr. and Mrs. Smith,

Thank you very much for posting your positive review on the Web site. One of my colleagues found your comment a few days ago. We rely on the support of loyal customers like you. We are waiting for you to visit us again.

By the way, could I include your review in our leaflet for the coming village festival? We would like to help the tourism association of Lawrence Village by distributing our leaflets to promote the festival.

We look forward to hearing from you soon.
Joanna Shane, Hamley's Bakery

Q21. What is Laurence Village well-known for?

(A) Local shops   (B) Mineral water

(C) Grain production   (D) Food factories

Q22. What is indicated about Hamley's Bakery?

(A) It is a family-owned business.

(B) It is conveniently located.

(C) It is closed on weekends.

(D) It is going to expand its parking space.

Q23. What is most likely true about Mr. and Mrs. Smith?

(A) They joined the factory tour.

(B) They live far from the station.

(C) They managed to get on the train.

(D) They uploaded their review to the Web site.

Q24. In the e-mail, the word "loyal" in paragraph 1, line 3, is closest in meaning to

(A) faithful   (B) potential

(C) upcoming   (D) delightful

Q25. What is mentioned about Ms. Shane?

(A) She belongs to the tourism association.

(B) She owns Hamley's Bakery.

(C) Her friends are arranging an event.

(D) Her coworker checked "Our Local Taste."

ボキャブラリーアルファ 13 Travel / Airport

この章のトピックでよく出る単語と表現です。日本語訳を見ながら英単語を声に出して言ってみましょう。

●旅行 / 空港のトピックに出てくる単語 CD 3-15

1 ☐ coincide [kòuinsáid]	動	同時に起こる、一致する
2 ☐ escort [éskɔː(r)t]	名	護衛、警護
3 ☐ depart [dipáː(r)t]	動	出発する
4 ☐ turbulence [táː(r)bjələns]	名	乱気流
5 ☐ embarkation [èmbɑː(r)kéiʃən]	名	乗船
6 ☐ valid [vǽlid]	形	確かな、正当な
7 ☐ transaction [trænzǽkʃ(ə)n]	名	取引
8 ☐ delay [diléi]	動	遅らせる
9 ☐ quarantine [kwɔ́rəntìːn]	名	検疫
10 ☐ blanket [blǽŋkit]	名	毛布
11 ☐ altitude [ǽltit(j)ùːd]	名	高度
12 ☐ destination [dèstənéiʃən]	名	目的地
13 ☐ thrill [θríl]	名	ぞくぞくする感じ、スリル
14 ☐ itinerary [aitínərèri]	名	旅行日程表
15 ☐ carousel [kærəsél]	名	回転式コンベア
16 ☐ excursion [ikskáː(r)ʒən]	名	小旅行、遠足
17 ☐ occur [əkáː(r)]	動	発生する
18 ☐ board [bɔ́ː(r)d]	動	乗船する、(電車、飛行機に)乗る

●旅行 / 空港のトピックに出てくる表現 CD 3-16

19 ☐ designated area	指定されたエリア
20 ☐ take out	持ち出す、取り出す
21 ☐ connecting flight	接続便
22 ☐ life jacket	救命胴衣
23 ☐ landing gear	着陸装置
24 ☐ jet lag	時差ぼけ
25 ☐ customs clearance	通関手続き
26 ☐ personal belongings	身の回り品
27 ☐ flag carrier	国を代表する航空会社
28 ☐ bus depot	バス車庫
29 ☐ International Date Line	国際日付変更線
30 ☐ boarding ramp	(飛行機などの) 移動式タラップ

UNIT 14 Housing / Construction

▶ Key Vocabulary 3-17

この章に出てくる下の英単語の中から日本語訳に当てはまる記号を（　）に記入しましょう。
答え合わせをしたら音声を聞いて英単語を声に出して読み、つづりを書き込み覚えましょう。

● 住居 / 建設のトピックに出てくる単語

1.	こする	（　）	9.	迅速な	（　）
2.	花柄の	（　）	10.	市営の	（　）
3.	舗装する	（　）	11.	（専門家）会議	（　）
4.	手押し車	（　）	12.	発音	（　）
5.	怒り狂った	（　）	13.	漏れ	（　）
6.	丈夫な	（　）	14.	下水	（　）
7.	育成する	（　）	15.	自発的な	（　）
8.	繁栄している	（　）	16.	故障	（　）

a. municipal	**b.** scrub	**c.** malfunction	**d.** consultation
e. wheelbarrow	**f.** voluntary	**g.** floral	**h.** thriving
i. durable	**j.** foster	**k.** leak	**l.** pave
m. furious	**n.** pronunciation	**o.** prompt	**p.** sewage

LISTENING SECTION

Strategy for Part 1 《写真描写問題の解き方》

主観的憶測はしない
下の Warming-Up の写真を見ながら選択肢が客観的かどうか判断しましょう。
● 写真を見ただけではわからない主観的なことや、個人的な憶測を含んだ選択肢は不正解になります。例えば、下の写真では労働者が住んでいる場所や、感情などは確認できないので、そのような表現を含んだ選択肢は不正解です。

 Warming-Up 3-18

音声を聞いて（　　　）内の語を穴埋めし、
正しい答えはどれか選びましょう。

(A) They are working on a (　　　　　) house.
(B) The carpenters are all very (　　　　　).
(C) The people are all wearing (　　　　　).
(D) Workers are (　　　　　) in a three-story apartment.

正しい答え　(A) (B) (C) (D)

133

▶ Part 1 Photographs

英文を聞き、4つの中から最も適切な描写を選びましょう。

Q1.

ⒶⒷⒸⒹ

Q2.

ⒶⒷⒸⒹ

Strategy for Part 2 ≪応答問題の解き方≫

否定疑問文など④　平叙文（疑問文でない設問の場合）

　設問が疑問文の形をしていない場合、「疑問詞だけを聞き取る」「動詞を聞き取る」など、聞き取りのポイントを絞ることが困難です。会話の流れをとらえ、話者の状況を想像しましょう。

Warming-Up 3-21

音声を聞いて、設問とその正解パターンの答えの意味を記入しましょう。

Q: Your new apartment has two bedrooms.

　（　　　　　　　　　　　　　　　　　　　　　　　　　　　　　　　　　　　）

A: Wow, that sounds wonderful!　　◎正解（　　　　　　　　　　　　　　）

A: How much is the monthly rent?　◎正解（　　　　　　　　　　　　　　）

A: That must be someone else's.　　◎正解（　　　　　　　　　　　　　　）

▶ Part 2 Question-Response

設問に対する応答として、最も適切なものを選びましょう。

Q3. Mark your answer on your answer sheet.　　ⒶⒷⒸ

Q4. Mark your answer on your answer sheet.　　ⒶⒷⒸ

Q5. Mark your answer on your answer sheet.　　ⒶⒷⒸ

Q6. Mark your answer on your answer sheet.　　ⒶⒷⒸ

Strategy for Part 3 《会話問題の解き方》

3人の会話問題③　will を含む設問

　Part 3 の設問のうち will や be going to を含むのは、3問中3問目の設問であることが非常に多いです。次に何をするかなど、会話文のあとに起こることについて問われたり、会話文の最新情報について問われたりします。従って、1問目、2問目を聞き逃しても会話文の最後の発言に集中すると3問目に正解する可能性が高くなります。

⬤ Warming-Up

次の設問を読んで、日本語に訳してみましょう。

　① What will Kate probably do next?

　（　　　　　　　　　　　　　　　　　　　　　　　　　　）

　② What will the man ask the woman to do?

　（　　　　　　　　　　　　　　　　　　　　　　　　　　）

▶ Part 3　Short Conversation

 3-26,27

会話文を聞いて、各設問に対する最も適切な答えを4つの選択肢から選びましょう。

Q7. Why does Catherine stay in the office?

　(A) She's furious about the noise.

　(B) She's talking with an accountant.

　(C) She's tired from aerobics.

　(D) She's worried about a complaint.

Q8. What does the man imply when he says, "So why don't we call it a day?"?

　(A) They should go home.

　(B) They should learn the pronunciation.

　(C) They should find a nickname.

　(D) They should check the exact date.

Q9. What will the man probably do tomorrow?

　(A) Sign a document

　(B) Look for a car-sharing business

　(C) Contact the real estate agency

　(D) Call a daycare center

「概要」と「詳細」③

　設問3問セットの中で、2、3問目に出題されることの多い『詳細問題』ですが、中でも3問目で多く出題される詳細問題があります。

　それは、トーク内の「～してください」というヒントを聞いて答える、**「話し手の依頼」に関する問題**です。ではこの「依頼」はなぜ3問目にくることが多いのでしょうか。

　TOEIC L&R のリスニング問題の大原則の一つは、**「設問の順序は、トーク内でヒントが登場する順序と同じ」**ことです。Part 4 では、トークの終盤に「～してくれませんか」という依頼が多く出てきます。よって、3問目の問題は「話し手の依頼」に関する問題が多くなるのです。

🌸 Warming-Up 💿 3-28

以下のような、Part 4 の「詳細を問う問題」が尋ねていることは何でしょうか。正しいものをそれぞれ1つずつ選び、○で囲みましょう。

　"What are the listeners asked to do?"（話し手・聞き手）の（依頼・申し出）

▶ Part 4　Short Talk

 3-29,30

説明文を聞いて、各設問に対する最も適切な答えを4つの選択肢から選びましょう。

Q10. Where is the announcement most likely taking place?

    (A) In a conference room

    (B) In a city hall building

    (C) At a construction site

    (D) At a furniture store

Q11. According to the speaker, what is the main feature of the facility?

    (A) It is more spacious than before.

    (B) It is made of natural resources.

    (C) It is conveniently located.

    (D) It is newly constructed.

Q12. What does the speaker imply when she says, "we'll see this district completely changed soon"?

    (A) The project will be completed.

    (B) The budget will be increased.

    (C) Many trees will be planted.

    (D) Someone will take her place.

READING SECTION

Strategy for Part 5 ≪短文穴埋め問題のための Grammar ≫

語彙問題②　単語の意味と文脈、前置詞との相性を理解しよう

　語彙問題では基本的に文脈を理解して正解を特定します。しかし、それぞれの品詞の性質によって、結びつきの強い単語との相性を考えることで、文脈を理解するプロセスを短縮することができます。つまり、他の単語との相性から正解を導き出すことで、文全体を読まなくても解答することができるのです。

☆動詞と前置詞との相性を覚えておこう

　前置詞の問題には Unit 9 で説明した**接続詞との使い分け**のほかに、**動詞とセットでの用法を問うもの**が多く語彙問題として出題されます。

- ●基本の前置詞　at「点のイメージ」, on「接触のイメージ」, in「包含のイメージ」
- ●自動詞とセットで使う一例

　accuse（人）of ...　　（人を…のことで責める）
　belong to ...　　　　（…に所属する）
　deal with ...　　　　（…を扱う）
　participate in ...　　（…に参加する）

☆形容詞と修飾する「名詞」の相性を考えよう

例えば、以下の空所に合う語を選ぶ場合、

They had to take an (　　) street when Water Drive was closed due to the accident.

(A) automated　「自動の」　　　　　**(B)** alternate　「別の」
(C) upcoming　「近く起こる」　　　 **(D)** ordinary　「普通の」

　選択肢は「形容詞」なので、次の名詞との相性を考えましょう。「別の道」にすれば、文脈に合うので **(B)** alternate が正解になります。

　その他に**動詞の場合、目的語との相性**を考えたり、**副詞の場合、修飾する「動詞」「形容詞」「副詞」との相性**を考えたりすることも正解への重要な手がかりです。

参考訳）ウォータードライブが事故で閉鎖していたとき、彼らは別の道を通らねばならなかった。

🔵 Warming-Up

通常、名詞が2つ続くと前の名詞が後ろの名詞を修飾して形容詞の働きをします。次の「名詞＋名詞」の表現の意味を下から選んで記号を（　）に記入しましょう。

(1) media scrutiny　　　（　　）　　(2) bank transfer　　　（　　）
(3) shipping charges　　（　　）　　(4) office supplies　　 （　　）
(5) customer satisfaction（　　）

　　a. 銀行振込　／　**b.** 事務用品　／　**c.** 送料　／　**d.** メディアによる精査　／　**e.** 顧客満足

▶ Part 5 Incomplete Sentences

空所に入る最も適切な語句を選びましょう。

Q13. Mr. Bell demanded that there should be electrical (　　) in every corner of the office.

(A) consents   (B) outlets   (C) powers   (D) switch

Q14. As (　　) in the specification document, please fill up the electric kettle when it is nearly empty.

(A) note   (B) noting   (C) noted   (D) notes

Q15. In order for prompt (　　) of your application to occur, please send us any additional documents as soon as possible.

(A) process   (B) processing   (C) processed   (D) and process

Q16. At the meeting the (　　) chairperson called for a vote on a reshuffle of top-ranking officials.

(A) presiding   (B) presides   (C) presided   (D) preside

Strategy for Part 6 ≪長文穴埋め問題の解き方≫

解答時間

　TOEIC L&R 対策で、「Part 6 は 10 分以内で解く」などとよく言われます。確かに Part 7 が 54 問あることを考えると、**Part 5 と Part 6 にかける時間は極力短くするべき**でしょう。では、Part 6 の文書を速く読むためには、どのような練習が効果的なのでしょうか。

　Unit 3 でも触れた通り、Part 6 の文書の大半は「100 語前後」です。皆さんも、速読の練習法について、色々と聞いたことがあるかもしれません。読解力には個人差もあるので、一概にこれが良いという方法はありませんが、例えば「文書をやや速めに 1 行ずつ指でなぞり、そのスピードで理解していく練習」や、「すでに意味がわかっている英文を何度も音読する練習」などは、リーディングのスピードを上げるのに大きく役立つと言われています。**色々な方法を試し、自分に有効な練習方法を見つけましょう。**

▶ Part 6 Text Completion

次の英文を読んで、選択肢の中から空所に入る最も適切な語句を選びましょう。

Remodeling of the Municipal Library

The City Office regrets to announce that the Municipal Library will be closed from next Monday ------ renovation, which is scheduled to be completed in early September.
17.

We have received many complaints and suggestions from library users, especially these last few years. The details of the plan ------ after consultations
18.
with various people, ranging from constructors to interior designers. ------ .
19.
Some of the main features of the ------ are as follows:
20.

1) The area of the floors will be nearly doubled.

2) The approach to the main entrance will have step-free access.

3) Some trees will be planted in the courtyard.

We apologize for any inconvenience the closure may cause you.

Q17. (A) on

(B) with

(C) for

(D) into

Q18. (A) have been finalized

(B) finalized

(C) was finalized

(D) have finalized

Q19. (A) They are now available on the city Web site.

(B) They are too busy to conclude planning by this month.

(C) They will be having some meetings with us.

(D) They will be on sale at bookstores next week.

Q20. (A) refund

(B) refurbishment

(C) reimbursement

(D) retirement

「TOEIC 漬け」でいい？

TOEIC L&R の学習を進める皆さんに質問です。「TOEIC L&R は楽しいですか？」

例えば、スコアが伸び盛りの方は楽しく取り組んでいることでしょう。さらに、「この文書には、こんな設問が合うかも」など、半ば問題作成者の視点で TOEIC L&R の世界に魅了されている方もいるかもしれません（いてほしいですが）。その一方で、スコアがなかなか上がらず、半ば嫌気がさしている方も少なくないかもしれません。また、気は進まないが、就職活動のために渋々取り組んでいる方もいることでしょう。

しかし実は、900 点以上の高いスコアを取っている人達の中にもこんな感想を持つ方が少なくないのです。「TOEIC は、会話や文書の内容が単調でつまらない」と。

皆さんにはぜひ高いスコアを取ってほしいと願う一方で、TOEIC が原因で英語そのものを嫌いになってほしくありません。TOEIC 対策とのバランスを取るためにも、映画やドラマ、音楽など、**自分の好きな分野の英語に触れる時間もぜひ大切にしてください**。

▶ Part 7 Triple Passages

次の英文を読んで、設問に対する答えとして最も適切なものを選択肢の中から選びましょう。

Periodic Checkup of the Apartment Building

The building manager would like to inform you that our apartment building will be having a periodic checkup on May 24. It is mandated that buildings of over five stories have to be inspected every three years. Although some equipment may be placed in the corridors, you will have nothing to worry about during the inspection.

As the building gets older, I have recently received more complaints about its facilities, such as water leaks, cracks in the floors, and elevator breakdowns. It seems now is the time for all residents to consider a major renovation for the building, and thus, I propose organizing a renovation planning committee to discuss the issues.

Thank you.

Allison Wells, Building Manager

E-mail

Dear Allison,

Thank you for taking good care of our apartment as always. As you pointed out in the notice, the building seems to have some problems, especially these last two years. I guess that the inspector will recommend replacing the sewage pipes and water-proofing the roof at least. While agreeing on the renovations, I am concerned how much they will cost.

Tony Brooks, Room 503

E-mail

Dear Tony,

I am glad to hear from you. I understand your concern with the cost and, if possible, I would like you to share your opinions with our committee members at our first meeting which is set for next weekend. Moreover, since we have so many issues to discuss, we would appreciate it if you could join the committee, too. It is voluntary and some of the other residents have already become members. If you are interested in joining us, please call me at extension 102 or just drop by my office during the daytime.
I look forward to hearing from you soon.

Allison

Q21. What is the purpose of the notice?
  (A) To notify the residents of an event
  (B) To ask the committee for assistance
  (C) To announce the period of the renovation
  (D) To organize a group of constructors

Q22. What problem is NOT mentioned in the notice?
  (A) Water leaks
  (B) Budget shortage
  (C) Floor damage
  (D) Elevator malfunctions

Q23. What is indicated about Mr. Brooks?
  (A) He has lived in the apartment for over two years.
  (B) He has inspected the property before.
  (C) He agrees with Ms. Wells on the costs.
  (D) He will attend the committee meeting.

Q24. What is most likely true about Ms. Wells?
  (A) She will attend the meeting on the weekend.
  (B) She is supposed to chair the committee.
  (C) She works for a building management company.
  (D) She has asked some constructors for an estimate.

Q25. What is implied about the renovation planning committee?
  (A) Its first meeting will be called in May.
  (B) Its members will receive some allowance for attendance.
  (C) It has a sufficient number of members.
  (D) It was established based on Ms. Wells' idea.

▶ ボキャブラリーアルファ 14 Housing / Construction

この章のトピックでよく出る単語と表現です。日本語訳を見ながら英単語を声に出して言ってみましょう。

●住居 / 建設のトピックに出てくる単語　CD 3-31

1 ☐ **option** [ápʃən]	名	選択肢、オプション
2 ☐ **indicator** [índikèitə(r)]	名	指標、サイン
3 ☐ **renew** [rin(j)úː]	動	更新する
4 ☐ **dimension** [dimén∫ən]	名	寸法、次元
5 ☐ **promptly** [prám(p)tli]	副	即座に、すぐに
6 ☐ **agent** [éidʒənt]	名	代理人
7 ☐ **site** [sáit]	名	敷地、地点
8 ☐ **adjacent** [ədʒéisnt]	形	近接した
9 ☐ **assist** [əsíst]	動	支える、手伝う
10 ☐ **occupy** [ákjəpài]	動	占める
11 ☐ **lease** [líːs]	名	賃貸契約、賃貸期間
12 ☐ **enhance** [enhǽns]	動	高める
13 ☐ **studio** [st(j)úːdiòu]	名	ワンルーム
14 ☐ **distinguish** [distíŋgwiʃ]	動	区別する
15 ☐ **fluctuate** [flʌ́ktʃuèit]	動	変動する
16 ☐ **collateral** [kəlǽt(ə)r(ə)l]	名	担保
17 ☐ **proximity** [praksíməti]	名	近接、近いこと
18 ☐ **comprehensive** [kàmprihénsiv]	形	包括的な

●住居 / 建設のトピックに出てくる表現　CD 3-32

19 ☐ **get out of**	逃げる、出る
20 ☐ **due to**	～のせいで
21 ☐ **down payment**	頭金、手付金
22 ☐ **power failure**	停電
23 ☐ **under construction**	工事中
24 ☐ **housing complex**	団地
25 ☐ **utility room**	家事室、小部屋
26 ☐ **durable years**	耐用年数
27 ☐ **land development**	土地開発
28 ☐ **installment plan**	分割払い
29 ☐ **fictitious company**	架空会社
30 ☐ **utility charges**	公共料金

LISTENING SECTION

▶ Part 1 Photographs

 3-33〜36

英文を聞き、4つの中から最も適切な描写を選びましょう。

Q1.

Ⓐ Ⓑ Ⓒ Ⓓ

Q2.

Ⓐ Ⓑ Ⓒ Ⓓ

Q3.

Ⓐ Ⓑ Ⓒ Ⓓ

Q4.

Ⓐ Ⓑ Ⓒ Ⓓ

▶ Part 2 Question-Response

 3-37～46

設問に対する応答として、最も適切なものを選びましょう。

Q5. Mark your answer on your answer sheet. Ⓐ Ⓑ Ⓒ

Q6. Mark your answer on your answer sheet. Ⓐ Ⓑ Ⓒ

Q7. Mark your answer on your answer sheet. Ⓐ Ⓑ Ⓒ

Q8. Mark your answer on your answer sheet. Ⓐ Ⓑ Ⓒ

Q9. Mark your answer on your answer sheet. Ⓐ Ⓑ Ⓒ

Q10. Mark your answer on your answer sheet. Ⓐ Ⓑ Ⓒ

Q11. Mark your answer on your answer sheet. Ⓐ Ⓑ Ⓒ

Q12. Mark your answer on your answer sheet. Ⓐ Ⓑ Ⓒ

Q13. Mark your answer on your answer sheet. Ⓐ Ⓑ Ⓒ

Q14. Mark your answer on your answer sheet. Ⓐ Ⓑ Ⓒ

▶ Part 3 Short Conversation

 3-47,48

会話文を聞いて、各設問に対する最も適切な答えを４つの選択肢から選びましょう。

Q15. Why has the woman come to Cube Pizza?

(A) To pick up food
(B) To sign up for membership
(C) To buy a ring
(D) To ask about the campaign

Q16. What is included as a special offer during the promotion?

(A) A Margherita pizza
(B) French fries
(C) Extra stamps
(D) A 20 percent discount

Q17. Look at the graphic. Approximately how much money has Ms. Ascough spent at this shop?

(A) $10
(B) $30
(C) $100
(D) $150

▶ Part 4 Short Talk

🎧 3-49,50

説明文を聞いて、各設問に対する最も適切な答えを4つの選択肢から選びましょう。

Q18. Who most likely are the listeners?

(A) Department managers

(B) Mechanical researchers

(C) Senior staff members

(D) New employees

Q19. What is not allowed during the lab tour?

(A) Leaving the group

(B) Taking pictures

(C) Touching the equipment

(D) Talking to the researchers

Q20. What are the listeners asked to do?

(A) Wear their badge

(B) Follow the schedule

(C) Ask questions

(D) Prepare for a meal

READING SECTION

▶ Part 5 Incomplete Sentences

空所に入る最も適切な語句を選びましょう。

Q21. Mr. Irving attended the ceremony on the 30th anniversary of the company at ( ) he gave a speech.

(A) where   (B) there   (C) what   (D) which

Q22. ABC airline has seen a ( ) increase in the number of customers.

(A) signify   (B) significance   (C) significant   (D) significantly

Q23. As of September 1, several of our engineers will be ( ) to Thailand.

(A) swiped   (B) transferred   (C) traveled   (D) progressed

Q24. While cash is our ( ) method of payment, there are other options available for your convenience.

(A) preferred   (B) prefer   (C) preference   (D) preferring

147

Q25. The private institution carried out a (　　) inquiry into the possibility of expanding the location.

(A) confident   (B) confidential   (C) confidence   (D) confidently

Q26. Some of the employees have (　　) with influenza during the past few weeks.

(A) fallen down   (B) taken on   (C) come down   (D) gone bad

Q27. To get to the supermarket, go (　　) the tunnel and turn left at the next traffic light.

(A) through   (B) download   (C) progress   (D) dig

Q28. Due to the extremely hot summer weather, some of the vegetables (　　).

(A) worsened   (B) ruined   (C) become old   (D) spoiled

▶ Part 6　Text Completion

次の英文を読んで、選択肢の中から空所に入る最も適切な語句を選びましょう。

New Continuing Education Program Starts!

You want to study on university campus again? Searching for a good place to study after work? Trent University can help you. We will be starting our ------- **29.** continuing education program, which has a variety of courses, in April. ------- **30.** . For the others, professionals from a variety of fields have been invited, such ------- **31.** lawyers, accountants, and interpreters. As all the lectures start after 6 P.M. and the campus is located near the station, you ------- **32.** rush to the classroom. All you need to do to apply for the program is visit the Web site www.trent.ac.nz and complete the online application no later than March 20.

Q29. (A) renewal   (B) renewing   (C) renew   (D) renewed

Q30. (A) Some of them will be provided by our professors.
(B) Some courses include 15 90-minute lectures.
(C) The admission office is located behind the East Building.
(D) You can pay the tuition by credit card.

Q31. (A) a   (B) as   (C) of   (D) that

Q32. (A) may want to   (B) don't have to   (C) will be able to   (D) aren't going to

▶ Part 7 Single Passage

次の英文を読んで、設問に対する答えとして最も適切なものを選択肢の中から選びましょう。

To: Elena Barton <elenabarton@wintech.co.ie>
From: Gillian O'Neil <gillianoneil@wintech.co.ie>
Date: November 17
Subject: My schedule proposal

Dear Elena,

Since the weather seems to be getting worse, we in the Human Resources Department may have to reconsider the schedule for tomorrow's internship orientation.

First, delays and cancelations have already occurred in public transportation. I think that most of the interns are using trains or buses so they probably won't make it in time for the ice-breaking session in the morning. - [1] -. The factory tour is scheduled for 11:00 A.M., isn't it? I'll ask the plant manager if it can be rescheduled for the afternoon just in case we can't start the session on time. - [2] -.

Next, I don't think the welcome party can be held in the garden due to the inclement weather. It is regrettable we can't have a barbeque outside for lunch, but what do you think about having an indoor party in the cafeteria instead? If you agree, could you check to see if it is still available?

Finally, having suddenly accepted two more interns yesterday, our department will need some additional laptop computers. Luke from your department is supposed to get them ready in the venue beforehand. - [3] -.

I hope my flight will be on schedule so that I can get back to the office this evening. - [4] -

Regards,
Gillian

Q33. What is the purpose of the e-mail?

    (A) To request permission for something

    (B) To suggest some schedule changes

    (C) To revise the budget plan

    (D) To update the interns about the event

Q34. The word "inclement" in paragraph 3, line 2, is closest in meaning to

    (A) bad   (B) windy   (C) cold   (D) humid

Q35. What is NOT mentioned about the orientation?

    (A) A welcome barbeque

    (B) A computer seminar

    (C) An ice-breaking meeting

    (D) A factory tour

Q36. What is implied about Ms. O'Neil?

    (A) She is the immediate supervisor of Luke.

    (B) She will be away from the office tomorrow morning.

    (C) She works in the other department than Ms. Barton's.

    (D) She is supposed to prepare some equipment.

Q37. In which of the positions marked [1], [2], [3], and [4] does the following sentence best belong?

    "Could you send him a reminder, please?"

    (A) [1]   (B) [2]   (C) [3]   (D) [4]

▶ ボキャブラリーアルファ 15 Mini Test

TOEIC 全体でよく出る単語と表現です。日本語訳を見ながら英単語を声に出して言ってみましょう。

● TOEIC 全体に出てくる単語　🎧 3-51

1 ☐ **result** [rizʌ́lt]	名	結果
2 ☐ **usually** [júːʒu(ə)li]	副	いつもは、たいていは
3 ☐ **evident** [évid(ə)nt]	形	明らかな
4 ☐ **mission** [míʃən]	名	使命、任務
5 ☐ **element** [éləmənt]	名	要素
6 ☐ **relatively** [rélətivli]	副	比較的に
7 ☐ **crosswalk** [krɔ́ːswɔ̀ːk]	名	横断歩道
8 ☐ **memorandum** [mèmərǽndəm]	名	社内回覧、事務連絡票
9 ☐ **consult** [kənsʌ́lt]	動	相談する、意見を聞く
10 ☐ **serious** [sí(ə)riəs]	形	深刻な
11 ☐ **detour** [díːtuə(r)]	動	迂回する
12 ☐ **concern** [kənsə́ː(r)n]	名	心配、懸念
13 ☐ **procedure** [prəsíːdʒə(r)]	名	手続き
14 ☐ **convenient** [kənvíːniənt]	形	便利な
15 ☐ **pertinent** [pə́ː(r)t(ə)nənt]	形	適切な
16 ☐ **refreshment** [rifréʃmənt]	名	軽い飲食物
17 ☐ **prohibit** [prouhíbət]	動	禁止する
18 ☐ **authority** [əθɔ́ːrəti]	名	権限、当局
19 ☐ **heartburn** [hɑ́ː(r)tbə́ː(r)n]	名	胸やけ
20 ☐ **plumber** [plʌ́mər]	名	配管工

● TOEIC 全体に出てくる表現　🎧 3-52

21 ☐ **branch office**	支店
22 ☐ **rat race**	いたちごっこ
23 ☐ **chronological order**	年代順
24 ☐ **certified mail**	配達証明付き郵便
25 ☐ **vicious circle**	悪循環
26 ☐ **biographical data**	個人データ
27 ☐ **towing charge**	移動料金
28 ☐ **excursion ticket**	周遊券
29 ☐ **carbon dioxide**	二酸化炭素
30 ☐ **secondhand store**	リサイクルショップ

TEXT PRODUCTION STAFF

edited by	編集
Masato Kogame	小亀 正人
Mitsugu Shishido	宍戸 貢

| English-language editing by | 英文校閲 |
| Bill Benfield | ビル・ベンフィールド |

| cover design by | 表紙デザイン |
| Nobuyoshi Fujino | 藤野 伸芳 |

| text design by | 本文デザイン |
| Nobuyoshi Fujino | 藤野 伸芳 |

| DTP by | DTP |
| ALIUS(Hiroyuki Kinouchi) | アリウス（木野内宏行） |

CD PRODUCTION STAFF

narrated by	吹き込み者
Jennifer Okano(AmE)	ジェニファー・オカノ（アメリカ英語）
Howard Colefield(AmE)	ハワード・コルフィールド（アメリカ英語）
Sarah Greaves(AsE)	サラ・グリーブス（オーストラリア英語）
Guy Perryman(BrE)	ガイ・ペリマン（イギリス英語）

PROGRESSIVE STRATEGY FOR THE TOEIC® L&R TEST
600点を目指すTOEIC® L&R TESTへのストラテジー

2021年1月20日　初版発行
2024年3月5日　第7刷発行

著　　者　　松本 恵美子
　　　　　　西井 賢太郎
　　　　　　Sam Little

発 行 者　　佐野 英一郎

発 行 所　　株式会社 成美堂
　　　　　　〒101-0052　東京都千代田区神田小川町3-22
　　　　　　TEL 03-3291-2261　FAX 03-3293-5490
　　　　　　https://www.seibido.co.jp

印 刷・製 本　　倉敷印刷株式会社

ISBN 978-4-7919-7233-3　　　　　　　　　　　Printed in Japan

・落丁・乱丁本はお取り替えします。
・本書の無断複写は、著作権上の例外を除き著作権侵害となります。